SILK PAINTING

The Artist's Guide to
Gutta and Wax Resist Techniques

SUSAN LOUISE MOYER

Photography by Dale E. Moyer

WATSON-GUPTILL PUBLICATIONS/NEW YORK

Art on first page:
Leland's Garden. © Sissi Siska. Photo by Carol Seitz.

Art on title page:
Day Lilies. © Susan L. Moyer.

Senior Editor: Candace Raney
Associate Editor: Janet Frick
Designer: Dale E. Moyer
Graphic Production: Ellen Greene
Text set in 10/12 Goudy

First published in 1991 in the United States by Watson-Guptill Publications,
a division of BPI Communications, Inc.,
1515 Broadway, New York, N.Y. 10036.

Library of Congress Cataloging-in-Publication Data

Moyer, Susan Louise.
    Silk painting : the artist's guide to gutta and wax resist
techniques / Susan Louise Moyer ; photography by Dale E. Moyer.
        p.   cm.
    Includes index.
    ISBN 0-8230-4828-4
    1. Silk painting—Technique. 2. Gutta-percha. 3. Resist-dyed
textiles. I. Moyer, Dale E. II. Title
ND1572.M68   1991
746.6—dc 20   91-14280
                                                        CIP

Distributed in Europe, the Far East, Southeast and Central Asia, and
South America by RotoVision S.A., 9 Route Suisse, CH-1295 Mies,
Switzerland.

Manufactured in Singapore

First printing, 1991

2 3 4 5 6 7 8 9 10/95 94 93 92

TO TINA AND DALE

Acknowledgments

First I would like to express my gratitude to my fellow silk painters who are featured in this book. Their thoughtful responses to my queries and their artwork made this project possible.

I would also like to thank my senior editor, Candace Raney, for providing the opportunity to create this book, and my associate editor, Janet Frick, for her careful editing and attention to detail.

I am indebted to Jackie Peters from the Jackie Peters Design Studio, Deborah Feinstein from D.F.S. Creative Consultants Ltd., and the staff working with the Aubergine Collection for lending me the designs from their collections.

Many thanks go to my silk-painting students from the Ridgewood Community School and the Old Church Cultural Center Art School for their enthusiasm and support. Special thanks to Joan Berglund for her helpful suggestions and ideas.

I am also grateful to Barbara Carr for her contribution to the section on silk and color.

For help with technical data, I would like to thank RoseMary Cohen from Atelier De Paris, Ken Steinmetz and Pierre Guidetti from Savoir-Faire, and last but not least, Susan Kocsis and Michael Katz from Rubert, Gibbon and Spider Inc.

Finally, I am especially grateful to my husband, Dale, for his photography and design of the book and for his friendship and support.

CONTENTS

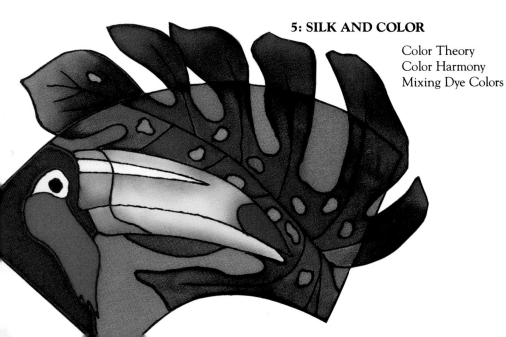

Jaguar. © *Cicely Gilman. Courtesy of the Barbara Aubergine Collection.*
This scarf is a beautiful example of the vivid colors achievable with French dyes.

INTRODUCTION

The intent of this book is twofold: to teach readers how to become skilled silk painters and to inspire them to learn. As an artist and teacher, I have presented in this book what beginning and intermediate silk painters need to know. I have provided them with the necessary information about the tools, techniques, and processes of silk painting so that they can become skilled at, and sensitive to, their craft. I have simultaneously tried to stimulate readers' creative imaginations by including rich and varied examples of silk painting by gifted artists whose work brings out all the beauty of the medium.

Once an artist has mastered the basic techniques of silk painting, these techniques can be applied to many types of art projects. The artists represented throughout this book use silk painting for commercial surface design, illustration, decorative art, and fine art. As commercial surface designers they use the medium to create the color and patterns that are printed on fabric, paper, and objects. Also, since silk is such a sensuous fabric, the medium naturally lends itself to wearable art and fine crafts.

There are several ways to paint on silk; each involves different materials, techniques, and processes. For the most part, this book focuses on the more traditional materials, such as gutta, wax, the traditional French dyes, and the newer Jacquard dyes formulated in the United States for silk painting. Understanding the techniques that use these traditional materials will let the reader explore many creative possibilities. It will also provide a baseline from which it is possible to explore and combine other materials and processes.

I would like to offer two general pieces of advice gleaned from years of teaching and from my own years of learning and growing as an artist. First: Silk painting is a very exciting, diverse, but temperamental medium. Therefore, as a novice, try not to embark on a project with a preconceived idea of what the medium can do for you; such a preconception may limit your silk painting experience and cause frustration. Instead, start by experimenting with the materials and techniques to discover their potential. (I also recommend that you read this entire book before starting *any* silk-painting project.) From this will come fresh ideas and the technical control you will need to successfully harness the medium for your individual artistic direction.

Second: By nature artists tend not to be joiners. As a result of this individualism and isolation, artists often find themselves reinventing the wheel or spinning their own wheels because they don't have the professional skills, connections, or technical information to advance in their specialty. Don't let this happen to you. If you have an interest in fabric and design and want to improve your skills, keep in step with the latest information and share ideas. You may seriously consider visiting your local library and consulting a recent issue of the *Surface Design Journal* for information on membership in the Surface Design Association Inc. This organization was established in 1977 out of a need to improve communication among artists, designers, members of the fashion industry, and educators working in textiles. Its members include artists working in various mediums such as painting, dyeing, printing, weaving, quilting, appliqué, and mixed media. The association provides a valuable forum where artists can exchange ideas and share information about the business, technical, and creative aspects of their profession. I have found its influence very helpful, and I suspect that many of you may also.

As a surface designer, teacher, and author, I sincerely hope that all the readers who interact with this book will be brought closer to their goals as silk painters and artists.

1: THE EVOLUTION OF A MEDIUM

Silk is a beautiful gift from nature that has been cultivated for over 3,500 years and enjoyed for over 4,000 years. Ancient colorants and resist techniques were developed to embellish the woven cloth of silk and cotton that came from India and China. The wax resist techniques of India have been documented back to the second century A.D. and 200 years later the wax techniques filtered into Java, which became the center of the batik industry.

Gutta is probably a more recent development in the history of resist techniques, but the origin of the craft remains something of a mystery. One could surmise that the craft has its origins in the Indonesian islands, where the pallaquium tree (from which gutta-percha is obtained) grows naturally. Resist techniques have long been part of the culture and industry of this region. There are a lot of unanswered questions about how the craft of silk painting spread to other parts of the world. Nevertheless, as a silk painter I find it very interesting to know about the more recent developments: how gutta and related techniques of silk painting eventually reached the United States and how this beautiful craft evolved into the diverse medium it has become today.

Coral Reef. © 1989 Joanne Siska. Photo by Joel J. Weissman.

A TECHNIQUE THAT TRAVELED ACROSS THE WORLD

Silk painters from France and Hungary report that their teachers acquired the skills and techniques of the craft in France from members of the Russian czar's family. During the Bolshevik Revolution, members of the czar's family dispersed. Many fled to Paris, bringing with them the secrets of silk painting using a substance called gutta, and introduced the process to Western Europe. Gutta is one of several linear barrier resists currently used in the process of painting on silk.

In the 1920s, unique fabric designs appeared in French haute couture. The silks from Lyon were of a fine, luxurious quality and embellished with beautiful hand-painted designs, many reflecting the influence of the art deco period. The French loved the sensuous hand-painted silks and turned what the French call the gutta serti technique of silk painting into a very profitable industry. Over the years the gutta serti technique of silk painting has become part of French culture and is considered a traditional French craft.

French kaftans and dresses of painted silk found their way to boutiques of avant-garde fashion in Greenwich Village in the late 1970s when most American artists were not privy to the secrets of the technique. Little if anything had been written about it, and the supplies were a mystery. American artists, enamored with painted silk, struggled to uncover tiny tidbits of information, barely enough to begin to experiment and discover the potential of the medium. Many artists have fascinating accounts of how they acquired their skills, but once the information started filtering into the community of artists, it came through several channels. One such channel is

an artist named Klara Gardon, who is one link to the development of silk painting as a medium for professional surface designers in America.

I visited Klara one afternoon and heard a rich and fascinating account of her life as a silk painter. Klara first became interested in the gutta resist technique of silk painting in 1936, when she traveled from her native town in Hungary to France. She fell in love with the unique hand-painted fashions in the Paris boutiques. During her stay she tried to find someone who would teach her the secrets of the mysterious resist. Unsuccessful in her search, she returned to Budapest, where she found a Hungarian artisan who, like the French artists, had learned this secret from members of the Russian czar's family. Klara, then a wealthy woman, offered to compensate him for his secret. To him it was priceless and not for sale.

Determined to learn this wonderful technique, Klara started to experiment with many preparations to find a resist pliable enough to hold up to the chemical dyes and alcohol, yet refined enough to draw delicate lines. Klara's living area, which was decorated with fine furnishings and hand-woven carpets, doubled as her chemistry lab. Once during her experiments, the flammable products caught on fire. The novice chemist managed to extinguish the flames. Klara tells how she, her mother, and her housekeeper cleaned up the mess, washed the walls, hung new drapes, and replaced a table and a valuable carpet. That evening's teamwork kept Klara's husband, who was not supportive of her hobby, occupied at the opera and a late-night cafe until the smoke cleared. But Klara was still as enthusiastic and determined as ever. She kept experimenting until she came extremely close to the formula, and then presented her findings to the Hungarian artisan. This time he felt that she had earned the right to know, so he sold her his formula for refining the gutta.

In 1951 Klara and her family were displaced from their home in Hungary and eventually emigrated to Israel in 1953. To help rebuild their lives, Klara used her talents as a surface designer to foster a new business. She had left Hungary an accomplished airbrush and batik artist who knew the secrets of the gutta resist. With these skills as a foundation she formed a studio in Israel with several other artists. Under her direction they produced exclusive hand-painted silk scarves.

Klara sold her business and in 1956 moved to Montreal to be near her son. The commercial climate there was not right for Klara's talents, so they moved to New York City in 1958. She took odd jobs in the textile industry until the late 1970s, when she began to work independently. She painted fabrics for fashion designers whose party dresses were sold through exclusive couturier shops on Madison Avenue, such as Lilli Rubin.

During that time Klara, who was always interested in fabric and design, would frequent a novelty fabric store on Broadway called Fun Fabrics. Jackie Peters, the proprietor of the shop, was fascinated by Klara and her hand-painted silk scarves.

Jackie had experience as a designer and stylist, and in 1978 she opened a surface design studio. The artists created original designs on paper for industrial printed textiles. At this time Jackie decided to study silk painting with Klara Gardon so that she could paint her original ideas on silk instead of on

Silk scarf © Klara Gardon. Collection of Yeshiva University Museum, New York. This is an example of Klara Gardon's work during the 1950s. She used gutta and applied dye directly to the fabric.

Surface design © Christa Van Valkenburg from the Jackie Peters Design Studio. This is a more contemporary use of silk painting to achieve a less structured effect. Notice how the dye is not always contained within a gutta line, but sometimes moves around it.

paper. "When you show an original design on silk," says Jackie, "it looks and feels as if it has already been printed." The presentation makes the design easier to sell. The Jackie Peters Studio became the first to produce a collection of designs on silk for the American textile industry, a revolutionary commercial idea that became very successful.

In 1982 another designer in Jackie's studio, studied with Klara Gardon. Sissi Siska found Klara, who was then in her seventies, to be an expressive, exuberant artist full of passion for her craft. "When you study with Klara," says Sissi, "you not only learn interesting silk painting techniques, but you are inspired and entertained through the richness of her life experiences."

SILK PAINTING AND MODERN SURFACE DESIGN

Within a year, other surface design studios began using silk painting, and a whole new way of presenting designs to the textile industry evolved. Professional art schools such as the Parsons School of Design, the School of Visual Arts, and the Fashion Institute of Technology hired silk painters to teach as part of their surface design curriculum. Jackie Peters was among them.

Many young, talented surface designers brought fresh ideas into the studios. The new silk collections created at this time reflect the interaction of these designers with the seasoned professionals who already had strong backgrounds in textile design.

The studio, the design experience, and the creative and competitive pressure to produce fresh new ideas for the textile and fashion industries were the ingredients needed to develop the medium of silk painting. This network of artists constantly investigated, explored, and manipulated the technique, sharing knowledge gained through their individual experience, until they mastered and developed silk painting into a versatile medium of artistic expression.

The designs featured in this book represent the work of those artists who were a part of this development. The specific designs were chosen not only for their artistic merit but to illustrate the potential of the materials and processes of silk painting.

This is a very exciting time for silk painters and other surface designers. Many have taken on the personal challenge of the fine arts and gallery shows, creating art to wear, receiving grants, organizing, teaching, and sharing ideas about silk painting in order to advance the medium.

Poisson Bleu. © Suzanne Punch. Here the artist used alcohol to move the dye around on the silk, creating a painterly effect. Suzanne used the alcohol technique to create a luminous, underwater look for her fish.

Underwater Film Fest. © Susan L. Moyer. This is a much more graphic approach to a similar theme. Because it was a surface design rather than a painting, it was kept much simpler so that it could be interpreted for printing onto fabric.

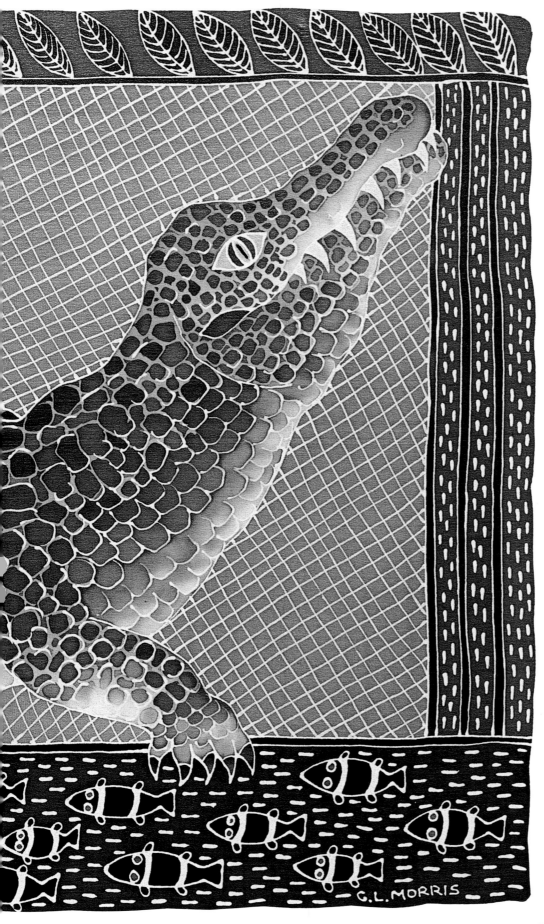

Baby Gator. © Gay Lynette Morris. This artist spent many of her younger years in Australia, so her images often reflect the strongly graphic aboriginal art she remembers from her childhood.

2: MATERIALS AND TOOLS

The silk painter needs some materials that are familiar to artists in other mediums (such as watercolor brushes and stretcher bars) and some that are unique to silk painting: gutta, dyes, dilutants, and of course the silks themselves.

The materials and tools that grow with us over many years take on special meaning for us. As artists we appreciate and respect these tools and materials because they take on specific roles as catalysts for our creativity. The unique images and enticing textures illustrated by the artwork in this book are examples of the traditional materials used for silk painting. Once you have become acquainted with the materials, tools, and processes demonstrated in this book, you will be better able to experiment with other newer products and add them to your creative repertoire.

NEW VERSUS TRADITIONAL MATERIALS

The recent interest in silk painting has generated a cornucopia of new products. In an effort to make silk painting easier and more attractive to the novice, many of these new products change the processes of silk painting. For example, water-based gutta eliminates dry cleaning but the resist will begin to dissolve with repeated applications of dye. Many of the dyes set by heat or chemicals are not as clear, bright, or versatile as the traditional dyes that require steam setting. Some fabric treatment products that retard the flow of dye are offered as an alternative to treating silk with gutta and solvent. These may be nontoxic and premixed, but they are not as effective and are incompatible with many silk painting techniques.

The new products are a welcome alternative for people who are doing simple craft projects or for art educators working with children. But these products may limit the potential growth of the professional artist and designer. It is very important to note that the silk painting tools and materials referred to in this book (unless otherwise noted) have stood the test of time and are compatible with the techniques and processes presented.

SILK FABRIC

Silk is absolutely unsurpassed as a medium for vibrant color. One of the many rewards of introducing silk painting to a group of artists is to feel their excitement as they discover the sheer beauty of the silk. No book can do it justice; you must see for yourself.

As transparent dye is applied, the color becomes an integral part of the silk. The fabric's luster and depth bring luster and depth to the colors. The drape of the fabric is flowing and the hand is warm to the touch, giving the color a sensuality. (Drape refers to how silk falls, and hand refers to how it feels to the touch.) The natural irregularities found in the silk filament give the color its unique sparkle and life.

The strength, elasticity, and durability of silk combine with its beauty to make it a perfect fabric for painting. It can be stretched, dyed, painted, batiked, washed, steamed, ironed, dry-cleaned, and still retain its natural beauty. Silk is resilient and durable enough to withstand all the processes involved in silk painting without being damaged.

There are two types of silk: cultivated and wild. The cultivated silk is preferred for silk painting. It is imported from China and other countries where labor is cheap and where the mulberry leaf, which is the diet of the cultivated silkworm, grows in abundance. For silk painters, the wild silks have a limited use but are still coveted for their natural beauty and irregularities.

As a child I was fascinated by the beautiful cecropia moth, whose caterpillar is light green with colorful stars adorning its upper body. This caterpillar eventually makes a cocoon by spinning a silk filament. As a child, I discovered two of these exotic caterpillars on a wild cherry tree at the edge of a nearby forest. I absolutely refused to relinquish my treasures back to Mother Nature. So, to appease me, and to make sure my caterpillars would have nourishment, my father dug up a wild cherry tree and tied it to a support post in our basement so the caterpillars could feed.

The last few days before the caterpillars spun their cocoons, they ate ravenously, day and night. They made loud chewing and tearing noises as they devoured every last leaf on the tree. We placed their cocoons in a dried flower arrangement. That winter they completed their metamorphosis. Spring arrived and as the moths emerged from their cocoons, they began exercising and drying their wings. What magnificent, perfect creatures they were, each with a wingspan of over 6 inches. Once strong enough, they flew to a screened window where they spent the night, attracting other cecropia moths. I was ecstatic. This incident began an interest in butterflies and moths that lasted for years.

The cecropia moth is only one of many North American moths that produce a silk filament. In the United States it is not economical to cultivate and produce enough cocoons to weave silk, so we import silk from the Orient. The best-known wild silks are the tussahs, imported from India and China, where women and children harvest and reel the cocoons. The color and quality of this silk varies and is determined by the climate, the soil, and the caterpillars' diet.

Unfortunately most wild silks are not suitable for silk painting because they are raw. Raw means that the silk has not been processed to remove the natural oils and gum. Therefore, the dye will not flow properly or be absorbed by the fibers.

If you have a passion for the color and texture of wild silks, purchase them from a reputable silk supplier and inquire about a particular silk's suitability for silk painting. To be safe, buy a sample piece of fabric and run a test before proceeding with a major purchase.

Cultivated silks have been processed and are ready for dyeing, and they have the purity and qualities that enhance color. Most cultivated silks are imported from Japan and China. In Japan the management and cultivation of the *Bombyx mori* silkworm and the mulberry tree on which it feeds are state of the art. It takes one acre of mulberry trees two seasons to produce 600 pounds of cocoons, which yield approximately 100 pounds of raw reeled silk plus some spinning fiber. The threads for weaving are made from eight to ten of the mile-long filaments that make up each cocoon. Silk filaments are stronger than any other natural or synthetic fiber, except nylon. The filaments are also very elastic and will stretch from 10 to 20 percent without breaking. This elasticity provides the silk with a "memory" that allows it to spring back into shape after being stretched, pulled, or crushed.

The weight of silk is expressed in a Japanese unit of measure called momme (mm). The momme range that is the most appropriate for the gutta serti technique of silk painting is eight to sixteen. An 8-momme silk is approximately 1 ounce per square yard. A 16-momme silk is approximately 2 ounces per square yard. Silks that are lighter than 8 mm are delicate and must be handled with care, especially when stretched in preparation for painting. When using heavyweight silks, the artist must thin the gutta so that it will penetrate the silk properly.

When selecting your silk for painting, purchase it from a supplier who services surface designers. The supplier should know the origin of the silks and their suitability for silk painting.

Butterflies (detail). © Sissi Siska. Photo by Carol Seitz. For this surface design of butterflies, the artist kept her approach as free-spirited as the butterflies themselves. The jacquard weave with its vertical stripes gives an extra textural dimension to the entire surface design.

To ensure that the dye will take evenly on the silk, most silk suppliers will recommend that you prewash their silks in Synthrapol, which is like a detergent but contains no alkali. (Alkali damages the silk fiber and dulls its natural luster.) Synthrapol, available from fiber arts catalogs, will remove any sizing or grease that repels the dye. When you have large quantities of silk to prepare for painting, bulk dry cleaning is a time-saving alternative to washing. After being dry-cleaned, the silk is wrinkle-free and ready to paint.

Caution: Most silks found in retail stores have been finished and will not accept the dye. A finish is any treatment given to a fabric after weaving to improve its appearance, marketability, and hand. Many of these finishes cannot be easily removed from the silk.

CARE OF SILKS

Silks are luxurious fabrics, delicate in an aesthetic sense yet practical and durable. With the proper care, silk fabrics can be enjoyed for a lifetime.

Unfortunately, since imported silk is often sold by weight, an old process of "weighting" woven silks with metal salts has given silk a reputation for poor durability. The metal salts coat the silk fibers, making them heavier and thus temporarily more profitable to sell, but later causing them to disintegrate and shred, creating a dry rotting effect that was blamed on mold, mildew, sunlight, and aging. Now that this "weighting" process is (for the most part) illegal, silk has proven to be very resistant to the various molds, mildews, and rots that plague other natural fibers. Even though silk is very resistant to decay, it should be stored in a cool, dry place, away from heat and dampness.

When storing silk yardage, roll it on a cardboard tube rather than folding it. Folds weaken the fibers, causing permanent creasing and eventual tearing.

To store clean pieces of silk, lightly layer them between sheets of nonacidic tissue paper or rice paper. If folding the silk is unavoidable, use the paper to support the folds to minimize creases. Place the layers of silk and paper in a cardboard box or wooden drawer.

Never use plastic for long-term storage; it does not allow the natural fibers to breathe, causing them to dry out and deteriorate. Plastic should be used only to transport silk and to temporarily protect work in progress from water spots, dye, grease, and dirt present in a studio situation.

If carpet beetles and mice are a problem in your area, periodically check your stored silk for signs of these pests. *Homo sapiens* is not the only species on earth that likes to line its nests with silk.

SILK WEAVES

Several types of silk weaves are suitable for silk painting. Each weave and weight has different qualities of drape, luster, texture, and durability; these are important considerations when choosing silk for a particular painting project. The following are several of the more common weaves used by silk painters.

Plain Weaves

Chiffon is a sheer, open plain weave with a soft hand. Painted chiffon is very popular for wearable art, especially for theater and dance costumes.

China silk, habutai, and pongee are tightly woven plain weaves. China silk is lightweight and very lustrous. The 5-momme China silk is fairly delicate and may snag or pull when it is being stretched, so handle it with extra care.

Habutai is fine and soft. Habutai originally meant silks that came from Japan, but now the terms habutai and China silk are occasionally used interchangeably to mean lightweight, plain woven silk.

Pongee is a plain weave of medium to heavy weight, heavier than habutai. It is stiff, tightly woven, and durable. The 12- or 14-momme pongee is an excellent choice if you plan to use the direct painting method described on pages 82–89. After a finished silk painting has been steamed and dry-cleaned, the hand of the pongee becomes much softer than before, and its luster improves with wear.

Pongee

Crepe de Chine

A luxurious surface to paint on, crepe de chine is the smoothest and most lustrous of all the crepes. The yarn is twisted before it is woven, and then the woven yardage is wet-finished to shrink the yarns and create a pebbly surface texture. This gives the crepe a durable textured finish and a stretchy hand. The weave accepts a lot of dye and takes it evenly, adding richness and depth to the colors. The elasticity of the weave gives crepe de chine a beautiful drape, making it a fine choice for wearable art.

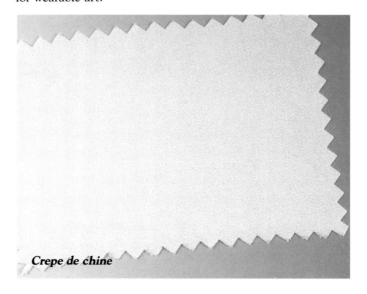

Crepe de chine

Charmeuse

Charmeuse is a finish that produces the highest luster and the smoothest hand of all the silks. The weave is durable but the finish can be bruised if not handled with care. Different types of charmeuse, such as crepe-back charmeuse and satin-back charmeuse, are distinguished by the weave found on the reverse side of the fabric. Lingerie charmeuse (12.5 momme) is lightweight; jacket-weight charmeuse (19.5 momme) is heavier. The charmeuse luster and sheen give brilliance to colors and the crepe gives it a sensuous drape. These qualities make it a fine choice for wearable art and decorative pillows.

Charmeuse

Jacquard

A jacquard is an elaborately woven fabric containing motifs and textures in the weave. Silk jacquards, in pure white, are available in a variety of different designs. They make beautiful grounds for decorative silk paintings because the woven pattern adds depth and interest to a design.

Jacquard

Silk Noil

When the silkworm is harvested it is allowed to create an escape hole in its cocoon. This breaks the continuous filament found in cultivated silks where the worm is not allowed to create an escape hole. The short fibers are then woven into a plain fabric called silk noil. You can distinguish silk noil from other silks by its natural off-white color, nubby flecks, muted luster, and rough texture. The natural-colored silk noil may often be confused with raw silk. Raw silk will not accept dye because it has not been degummed, but a degummed and bleached silk noil will take dye beautifully and can be an alternative for those who like the natural qualities of wild silk. Although the rough texture created by the pieces of cocoon left in the noil and the nubby fibers make this fabric unsuitable for delicate gutta lines, it is a perfect choice for ethnic batiks. The color of some silk noils is tan, a neutral ground, which you should take into consideration when mixing colors. Because the fibers of silk noil are short, the woven fabric is not as durable as other silks.

Caution: To avoid confusion, always inquire about the fabric. Test a sample to determine whether or not it has been degummed and will accept the dye.

Silk noil

Silk Scarves

Scarves are fabulous for silk painting. Imported scarves—usually made of china silk, crepe de chine, or charmeuse—are individually hemmed by laborers who use a traditional hand-rolling technique practiced at scarf manufacturing communes in China. Each individual worker produces only four to ten scarves a day. Purchasing the scarves with edges already finished is efficient and less costly than contracting or trying to do such fine hand-finishing yourself.

SILK DYES

Shimmering color, which is the hallmark of silk painting, is achieved by the use of dye. Dyes are translucent and when applied to silk become an integral part of the sensuous fabric.

Dyes should not be confused with fabric paints, which contain binders and extenders that render them opaque. When paints are applied to silk they change the drape, texture, and hand of the fabric, masking its natural beauty.

The dyes used in the artwork and demonstrations presented in this book are primarily from two manufacturers. One is Sennelier, which produces Super Tinfix and Tinfix, and the other is H. Dupont. The Super Tinfix dyes were developed in France in the 1960s for silk painting so that designers could create scarf prototypes on silk instead of paper. The French dyes are clear and bright. Their hues are close to true primaries, so they mix predictably to form new colors. It naturally follows that American surface designers, who design prints for the fashion industry, would favor these dyes. Super Tinfix dyes are very concentrated and intended for professional use; they are used by many designers as stock dyes from which they mix each season's color palette. The Tinfix line is less concentrated and includes a wide variety of colors that have been mixed from the Super Tinfix dyes.

The French dyes belong to a group of dyes that were developed primarily for protein fibers such as silk and wool. They are ink dyes in a slightly alcoholic solution and are considered nontoxic. The alcohol is added to produce more vivid color and to help the liquid dye flow on the silk. These dyes are painted directly onto the fabric and require a concentrated bath of steam and heat to be fixed. Steam fixing or setting is done in a steamer.

Even though these dyes are considered nontoxic, they should be handled with protective gloves and clothing because they will stain skin and clothing. The cleansers needed to remove the stains are harsh on your hands.

The manufacturers recommend that the dyes be stored in a cool, dark place, where they will have a shelf life of approximately two years. I have stored these dyes for longer than two years and have found most of the colors remain stable, but if the dye separates in the bottle or thickens, it has lost its effectiveness.

Since the Sennelier dyes (Tinfix and Super Tinfix) and H. Dupont dyes can be mixed together, I stock my studio with a selection of colors from both companies. The colors I work with are based on economy, color theory, convenience, and availability.

Prepackaged dyes in small quantities are very costly, so I buy quantities of a select group of colors and then mix others from them. For a list of these colors, see page 61.

When working with dyes and reflective materials such as silk, the artist uses the subtractive primaries to mix all the colors. The three subtractive primaries (also known as process colors) are the most important: clear yellow, cyan (process blue), and fuchsia (magenta).

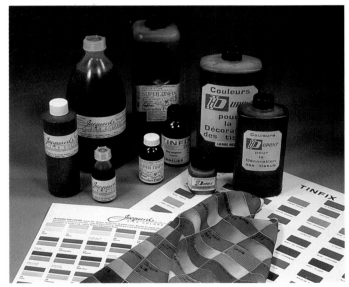

From right to left are the French dyes (H. Dupont, Tinfix, and Super Tinfix) and the Jacquard silk colors with their green labels. Each brand is packaged in various quantities. Printed color charts are often available on request. Some suppliers, representing an individual brand of dye, sell their own color charts painted on silk, and these charts represent color more accurately than those printed on paper. The silk chart pictured here represents Super Tinfix, Tinfix, and H. Dupont and was executed by me as a studio reference.

Sennelier dilutant, H. Dupont dilutant, and isopropyl alcohol are mixed with distilled water and are used to dilute the French dyes. Water, preferably distilled water, is the dilutant for the Jacquard silk colors. After mixing the dilutants with the appropriate amount of distilled water, I recommend putting the mixture in a handy squeeze bottle.

DILUTANTS

The H. Dupont, Tinfix, Super Tinfix, and Jacquard dyes can be diluted in various percentages. For example, Super Tinfix dyes can be diluted up to 2 or 3 times their strength and still retain their intensity and brilliance. When working with Super Tinfix dyes, you must remember that more dye does not always make a color brighter or deeper. Without the addition of a dilutant, some of the colors may become harsh or dull when steam-set. The extra color may bleed during the steaming process and run if the fabric is washed.

By diluting a dye even farther, you will produce tints and tones. You can mix your own dilutant from isopropyl alcohol and distilled water. The alcohol is a diffusing agent that helps the dye spread evenly on the silk. It also acts as a drying agent that speeds up the process of silk painting. Too much alcohol will break down a gutta line. Therefore, also add water to cut the strength of the alcohol. Water also keeps the fabric wet, allowing you more control of dye application—especially in large areas and backgrounds. Dyes can be affected by the chemicals and minerals found in tap water, so it is best to mix your dilutant with distilled water.

The proportions of alcohol to distilled water vary depending on the percentage of alcohol already found in the brand of alcohol you purchase. You can also vary the percentage of alcohol to water to adjust for technical considerations. More water keeps the fabric wet longer. More alcohol makes the dye spread faster and dry more quickly. Depending on the nature of your painting project, you might prefer one condition or the other.

Suggested dilutant formula for the brands of alcohol with a 70 percent alcohol content:
⅔ alcohol to ⅓ distilled water (dries more slowly)
¾ alcohol to ¼ distilled water (dries faster)

Suggested dilutant formula for the brands of alcohol with a 90 to 95 percent alcohol content:
½ alcohol to ½ distilled water (dries more slowly)
⅔ alcohol to ⅓ distilled water (dries faster)

Very light tints and tones have a tendency to dry unevenly when applied to large areas. This is especially true on lighter-weight silks. To help alleviate streaking, and as an alternative to alcohol, use the Tinfix diffusing agent or the H. Dupont dilutant. These dilutants are nontoxic and odorless, and they can be mixed with either brand of dye. These dilutants make the dye flow and dry more evenly. Also, because these dilutants do not contain alcohol, they will not break down thin gutta lines or cause irritation to the few silk painters who are sensitive to the alcohol fumes.

The mixing of dilutant to distilled water varies considerably with the manufacturer, so be sure to inquire about this when you purchase the product.

GUTTA AND GUTTA-LIKE RESISTS

Gutta and similar resists are usually applied to the silk in a linear manner, and their primary job is to control the flow of dye by delineating and separating areas of color. The resist lines penetrate and seal the silk fibers, creating a barrier that contains the flow of the liquid dye.

Clear Gutta

Most of the artwork featured in this book was executed with gutta, which is the linear resist preferred by professional silk painters. The raw gutta, also called gutta-percha, is a coagulated milky latex substance collected from a hybrid species of the palaquium tree, a tropical tree grown on plantations in Peninsular Malaysia, Borneo, and Sumatra. In order to make a gutta resist, which is a clear thick liquid, this milky substance is put through a refining process. Once the gutta is refined and applied to the silk, it dries as a rubbery pliable line. After a painting is finished and the dyes have been steam-set, the gutta can be removed from the silk with dry-cleaning fluids. Whether clear gutta is applied over white silk or a colored ground, that underlying color will remain after the gutta is removed.

Black and Colored Guttas

Sennelier makes permanent gutta in several colors. When permanent gutta is dry-cleaned, the gutta itself is removed, but its color remains in the fabric. Therefore, clear gutta and

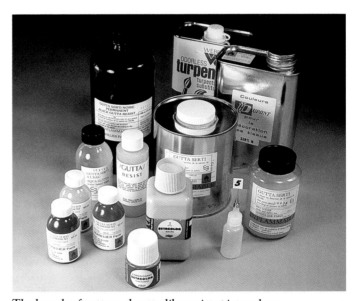

The brands of gutta and gutta-like resists pictured are Sennelier, H. Dupont, Jacquard, and Setacolor by Pēbēo. Each brand of resist is available in various quantities. These solvent-based resists are thinned to the proper consistency for application with Turpenoid. The French Setacolor Pearl fabric paints are dry-cleanable metallics that can be applied as decorative linear resists. The clear water-based resists are available in H. Dupont, Jacquard, and the Sennelier brand pictured. Plastic gutta applicators like the one pictured can be fitted with various sizes of metal tips.

Reef Heron. © *Gay Lynette Morris. For this large painting, the artist worked with permanent black gutta to produce a stylized tropical look.*

colored guttas can be used in the same painting to achieve various effects. The color stays and the clear gutta is removed. Also, if only black or colored guttas are used, the silk will not necessarily need to be dry-cleaned.

Sennelier permanent gutta comes in black, red, blue, yellow, and green. The colored guttas (but not black) can be mixed together to produce other colors. It is important to note that the quality and consistency of the permanent black gutta varies. This could discourage a novice silk painter. Therefore, I recommend that novices wait until they are familiar with the qualities of a good, clear gutta resist before working with the black gutta.

Water-Soluble Resists
Water-soluble resists can be washed out of the silk after the dyes have been steam-set. Although this eliminates dry cleaning, most water-based resists do not give the linear control needed to achieve professional results, and they limit the versatility of the medium. This is especially true with layering and overdyeing techniques for which a hard-edged resist line is important. The repeated application of dye and alcohol dilutant will break down a water-soluble resist. Be forewarned that when you are overdyeing colors, the water-soluble resists tend to lift some of the color out of the silk when they are removed, leaving a lighter line of color. Also, some of these resists need hot water and scrubbing to be removed from the silk. During this process the dyes may lose some color intensity.

As an alternative to gutta, some artists use water-soluble resists such as Sennelier Aqua Gutta to create textures. When gutta is applied over a large surface, as opposed to being used for line work, the fumes from the solvent become intolerable. The water-soluble guttas do not emit such fumes. If necessary, they can also be removed from the silk by dry cleaning.

Redans. © Suzanne Punch. Water-soluble gutta helped the artist create interesting textures in this large abstract painting. Water-based gutta is preferred for this type of work because it doesn't expose you to the fumes found in solvent-based gutta.

Textured Stripes. © Susan L. Moyer. *The texture of this surface design was created by using a small sponge to apply successive layers of gutta between applications of dye.*

Golden Orchids. © Susan L. Moyer. *The beauty of metallic gutta is clearly evident here. Because this was a surface design, my concern was with the visual result and not the durability of the resist. For wearable art, where durability counts, try experimenting with Jacquard metallic resists.*

Metallic Resists

There are several very beautiful and effective silver, copper, and gold metallic guttas and gutta-like resists on the market. Unfortunately the true metallics are not permanent, which means that the metallic look will be removed with the gutta if the silk is dry-cleaned. There are permanent metallic gutta-like resists, but many artists find the gold and silver to be off in color and not as bright as the metallic guttas. Even though these permanent gutta-like resists are not as bright as the metallic guttas, very beautiful results can be achieved with them.

In an effort to keep all the resist products and processes applicable to dry cleaning, you may consider using Setacolor Pearlescent fabric paints, manufactured by Pēbēo in France. These fabric paints are permanent and come in a variety of iridescent colors. The colors and binders remain in the silk when it is dry-cleaned or washed, so the inherent stiffness of these metallic paints also remains in the fabric.

In order to apply these fabric paints as a resist, you must mix them with a small amount of Setacolor thickener. The thickener creates the proper consistency for fine line work. To achieve a reversible fabric and to ensure an effective resist barrier on heavy fabrics, apply the paint to the back side of the fabric as well as the front. This second application can be applied before or after the first application dries; just be careful not to smear any wet paint. Before applying the dye, allow the paint to dry thoroughly. Then heat-set the resist with an iron by carefully following the manufacturer's instructions.

Rain on Catfish Billabong. © *Gay Lynette Morris. Gay often uses clear gutta as a strong design element that gives her silk paintings their unique style. The black stems in this design were applied before the raindrops of clear gutta.*

PREPARING GUTTA FOR APPLICATION

Gutta can vary in thickness from container to container. Therefore, until you are experienced, you must test your gutta to see if it is the proper consistency for the particular weave and weight of your fabric. To test the consistency of the gutta, fill a resist applicator at least three-quarters full with gutta. Draw an enclosed shape on a scrap of silk. The gutta should be fluid enough to flow easily when the applicator is squeezed lightly, and it should penetrate the silk front to back. Check the back of the fabric against the light to see whether the gutta has penetrated properly.

If the gutta has not penetrated, either your lines are too thin or the gutta is too thick. To adjust the weight of your lines, draw more slowly and squeeze the gutta applicator more firmly. To adjust the consistency of the gutta, thin it with a solvent such as mineral spirits, turpenoid, or gutta solvents offered by Sennelier and H. Dupont. Fill an 8-ounce (240-ml) glass jar with approximately 6 ounces (180 ml) of gutta. Add 1 teaspoon (5 ml) of solvent and shake the capped jar vigorously. Before filling your resist applicator, let any air bubbles that have formed in the jar rise to the surface and escape.

With the resist applicator, test the consistency of the gutta again by drawing an enclosed shape on your silk. Make any adjustments to the 6 ounces (180 ml) of gutta by adding 1 teaspoon (5 ml) or less of solvent at a time, shaking the jar after every addition of solvent. Once the gutta is penetrating the silk properly, let it dry 10 to 20 minutes. Then test its strength as a resist by applying dye within the enclosed shape. If the resist barrier holds the dye from escaping the enclosed shape, your gutta is the proper consistency to apply to the silk.

If the gutta is too thin, the resist line spreads slightly on the silk, causing ragged edges and thin areas where the dye will seep past the barrier. To remedy this you can add more gutta or leave the cap off your gutta applicator long enough for some of the solvent to evaporate. For more information on applying gutta, refer to pages 47–48.

Assembling the Applicator

Gutta and gutta-like resists are applied to the silk with small squeeze bottles made of soft plastic, called gutta applicators. Each applicator comes with a metal tip that has been threaded so that it will screw onto the cap of the plastic applicator. The metal tips come in sizes 3 (the smallest), 5, 7, and 9. Size 5 is the most popular and recommended for the novice.

Although the applicators and metal tips can be purchased separately and are meant to be interchangeable, most artists find that constant removal of the metal tips from the plastic weakens the grooves and subsequently loosens the metal tips. Therefore, having one plastic squeeze bottle for each tip is advisable. Since the metal tips are screwed onto the caps of the applicators, all the artist needs to do is switch caps to accommodate a gutta-filled applicator with a variety of metal tip sizes. It is also more efficient to have a separate applicator for each gutta type and color.

Once the tip is in place, insert the straight pin that comes with the applicator into the metal tip and pierce the plastic. Push the pin in and out of the tip several times to make sure the opening is clear. To keep track of this tiny pin (especially size 3, which is smaller than your average silk pin and thus difficult to replace), create a flag by placing a colored piece of tape around the pinhead. You can also write the size number on this flag. When the applicator is not being used, keep the gutta from drying and clogging the opening by storing the pin in the metal tip.

Filling the Gutta Applicator

To fill an applicator from a container of resist, hold the open container about 4 inches above the applicator. Pour the resist in a thin stream into the applicator until the applicator is three-quarters full. Then, in one continuous motion, twist the container and tip it upright so that the stream breaks and the resist draws back into the container. If coordinating this proves difficult, place a small funnel in the applicator and then pour the resist.

Holding the container of gutta above the gutta applicator, slowly pour the gutta in a thin stream, filling the applicator at least three-quarters full.

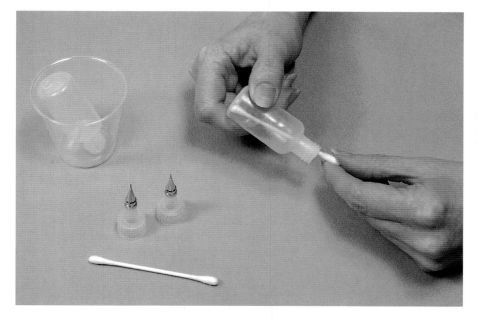

Here you see one gutta applicator air-drying and another being cleaned with a cotton swab. Two metal applicator tips rest upright on the table.

Cleaning and Storing the Gutta Applicator

Never leave gutta (or gutta-like resists) in the applicator more than one or two days. The solvent in the gutta will dissipate through the porous plastic, leaving the gutta in a hardened state. To avoid this, either store a gutta-filled applicator in a tightly capped jar of solvent, or decant the gutta by unscrewing the cap and pouring what you can back into its original container. After decanting the gutta, lean the gutta applicator open side down against the inside of a small jar or disposable cup and let it air-dry a day or more. Once the gutta is dry, take a cotton swab and twist it inside the applicator to pull the film of dry gutta off the inside. Continue twisting until you have pulled the thin film of gutta away from the sides and out of the opening. Do the same with the applicator top. This technique makes it very easy to remove gutta from a resist applicator. To be efficient, I suggest keeping two or three applicators handy so one can be drying while another is being used.

If you are working with a water-soluble gutta, you can store the applicator in a jar of water or pour the remaining resist back into its original container. Then immediately rinse the applicator and the metal tip thoroughly in water.

TIPS

• Never mix your gutta with more than one solvent.

• It is easier to control the flow of gutta if the resist applicator is at least three-quarters full.

• Heat thins gutta and humidity dampens the silk, preventing the gutta from sealing its fibers. Therefore, when applying gutta under hot and humid conditions allow it to dry 15 to 20 minutes and test the resist with a wash of dilutant before applying dye. If the climate in your area is humid or damp, you may need to dehumidify your work area before working successfully with gutta.

• Black gutta that has not been air-dried can backstain during dry cleaning and smear when ironed. Therefore, after steam-setting the dyes, let black gutta cure three or more days before dry cleaning, and iron the painting by placing it between two layers of clean newsprint.

• If the gutta thickens after one or two days in the plastic resist applicator, use an eye dropper to add a few drops of solvent. Shake the applicator well. Then allow any air bubbles in the gutta to rise and escape before testing your resist. If the gutta has completely hardened, fill the applicator with solvent, cap it, and let it sit for a few days. The gutta will soften so that you can pull it out in one lump and discard it. Try to avoid this. It is a messy job that requires wearing rubber gloves and wastes time, gutta, and solvent.

STORAGE TIPS

• Store gutta at room temperature but avoid extremes. Gutta should never be allowed to freeze or be exposed to temperatures over 100 degrees. It will break down, become very runny, and lose its resist qualities if it freezes or becomes overheated. To avoid overheating gutta during hot weather, keep it in the refrigerator. Gutta that is thin and will not thicken when the solvent is allowed to dissipate is spoiled and should be discarded.

• The solvents in gutta are flammable and toxic. Store gutta in a glass jar or in its container away from a heat source. The solvents turn to vapors very quickly, so work in a well-ventilated area equipped with an exhaust fan. Keep gutta containers tightly capped.

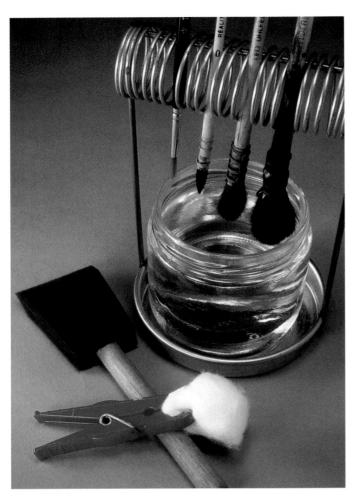

A brush holder is a convenient place to rinse and hang your brushes while painting. From left to right in the holder: small Prolene watercolor round and three sizes of squirrel-hair quill brushes. In front of the holder: sponge brush and cotton puff in clothespin.

To clean a squirrel-hair quill brush thoroughly, wet a bar of Ivory soap and hold it in the palm of your hand or put it in the sink. Point the brush directly into the bar of soap so that the hairs form a flat circle and the ferrule is up against the bar. Twirl the brush back and forth to the left and right until you see a colorful pattern. Then rinse the brush and repeat the process until the brush rinses clean.

SILK-PAINTING BRUSHES AND THEIR CARE

The types and sizes of brushes a silk painter may use are dictated by the medium as well as by each artist's creative needs. The following brushes and implements have been found to be very suitable for the different technical considerations encountered when applying liquid dye.

Squirrel-hair quill brushes hold a lot of dye, come to a fine point, and are resilient. They are excellent for painting backgrounds that border intricate areas and for blending color on the silk but are not recommended for enclosed, detailed areas. A squirrel-hair quill brush may let go of too much dye, causing the dye to flood and run over a resist barrier. Since small Prolene and sable watercolor rounds do not hold as much dye as a squirrel-hair quill, they are preferable for applying flat color or for shading and blending color in small, enclosed areas.

Prolene watercolor rounds are made of a synthetic hair that holds up well to the drying effects of dye and alcohol. These fine brushes don't hold as much dye as squirrel hair, but they are excellent for shading and blending color in small motifs. They are slightly stiffer than the squirrel-hair quill brushes, which makes them excellent for rub-blending. The synthetic hair is easily rinsed and cleaned between colors in a container of water or alcohol dilutant.

The brushes used for silk painting must be carefully cleaned so that future applications of dye will not be contaminated by streaks of unwanted color. When you are in the process of painting and need to clean a brush, first rinse it in a large container of water to remove most of the dye and then in a small container of isopropyl alcohol. Blot the brush and ferrule on a paper towel and continue painting.

Since dyes and alcohol are harsh and drying to natural sable and squirrel hair, these brushes must be given special care so that they will retain their shape and resilient spring. Therefore, when you are finished painting or if you need to thoroughly clean a brush, wash it with a bar of Ivory soap, as shown in the illustration below. The soap will remove the dye and leave the brush hair soft and resilient. After cleaning, let the brush dry suspended in a brush holder so the brush does not touch a surface and become misshapen.

Since large squirrel-hair quill brushes are the most difficult to clean, save yourself the trouble by using a foam brush or cotton puff whenever you can. These implements are handy for painting large areas and backgrounds that do not border an intricate design. The foam brushes are not easily cleaned, but thorough cleaning is unnecessary if you have one of these inexpensive brushes for each color family plus one for yellow and one for black. Better yet is a cotton puff held in a plastic clothespin. I know this doesn't look like a very professional implement, but don't let it fool you. The cotton moves easily on the silk and applies color evenly. Leftover dye can be squeezed back into a jar, and the cotton can be discarded, making clean-up a snap.

Special Tools for Wax Resist Techniques

Certain additional tools and supplies are needed for wax resist techniques: paraffin, beeswax, an electric wax pen, and an electric tjanting. To find out more about these materials, refer to pages 94–95.

Before storing a brush, remove any excess water and re-form the point. To do this, shake the brush down toward the floor or into the sink. If the point doesn't take shape by itself, form it with a little Ivory soap, which you can rinse out just before you use the brush again.

THE SILK PAINTER'S STUDIO

A well-equipped studio makes it much easier and more comfortable for any artist to work with silk, gutta, and dyes. Studio space is important to any artist, but the silk painter needs several things in particular: balanced lighting, working surfaces that will not be damaged by the working materials, and adequate ventilation.

Lighting

Color is determined by how much of the full spectrum of white light an object absorbs and how much it reflects back to our eyes. Dyes make silk absorb more wavelengths of light, so that only part of the spectrum is reflected back to us; for this reason dyeing silk changes its color.

It is important to remember that color is affected by the nature of the lighting source. That is, the same dye will seem to be a different color under cool lighting (leaning toward blue) than under warm lighting (leaning toward red). We judge the color only by what wavelengths of light reach our eyes, not by whether the original lamp gives out truly white light or not.

Balanced-spectrum fluorescent lighting has been developed for graphic and art studios. It gives the truest color, so it is ideal to work with when mixing, matching, and creating color. The fluorescent bulbs can be installed in a ceiling fixture measuring 1 foot by 4 feet, or a work surface can be spotlighted by coordinating a desk lamp with bulbs of various sizes. In either case, check the availability and size of the bulbs before purchasing a fixture.

Another option is to combine a warm incandescent light with a cool fluorescent light to produce what is referred to as a blended light.

No matter how carefully you plan the lighting of your work area, on occasion there will be discrepancies when you match colors. Sometimes the colors of two fabrics will seem to match under either incandescent or fluorescent lighting but not in daylight or full-spectrum light. Often this is because the dyes used for man-made fibers are different from those used for nat-

ural fibers, and they react differently under various kinds of light. This phenomenon is called metameric color. Even if you can't perfectly match some other piece of fabric, rest assured that the same dyes will produce the same color on the same piece of silk.

Color in the Studio

When you are working with color and making color decisions, the colors of your working environment should be neutral. Matte or semigloss white walls diffuse the light and cut glare; either type of paint combined with balanced-spectrum fluorescent lighting minimizes eye fatigue, and creates a very cheerful and productive working environment.

Working Surfaces

Porous surfaces such as composition vinyl, some paints, cement, tile grout, wood, and rugs will absorb dye and may become permanently stained. To protect these surfaces, cover the work area and floor with a thick plastic drop cloth or oilcloth. Wipe up any spills and drips as they occur so that you do not accidentally track them into unprotected areas.

If you have the option, test any new surfaces for resistance to dye stains before they are installed. You may consider a black floor, which will not show dye stains and has the added plus of being a neutral color in the studio environment.

Stainless steel sinks are the best for silk painters because they will not react with or absorb dye.

Ventilation

When working with solvents, wax, gutta, and any potentially toxic materials, make sure to ventilate your work area properly. Place an exhaust fan in front of your work table either in the wall, window, or ceiling so that the fumes are drawn away from you and vented outside. Do not position an exhaust fan in any way that it will draw the fumes past your face, such as behind or directly above you. If possible, open a window to keep fresh air moving through the room.

3: PREPARING THE SILK FOR PAINTING

The choice of frame and securing device that will work best for stretching a particular piece of silk depends on your individual requirements and the nature of your project.

Before you can paint on silk, the silk must be measured and torn to the size you need, suspended above your work surface, and stretched evenly and tautly on a frame. A variety of frames are available, as well as a selection of devices for securing the silk to the frames. Some silk painters use a harite and a set of shinshi, exotic stretching devices that come from the Orient and are as exotic as the silks themselves. Others use more commonplace equipment like ordinary canvas stretcher bars or even sawhorses from a hardware store.

Preparing the silk properly may seem like a mundane aspect of the silk painting process, but it is crucial to the success of your final project.

Forest Floor. © *Sissi Siska.*

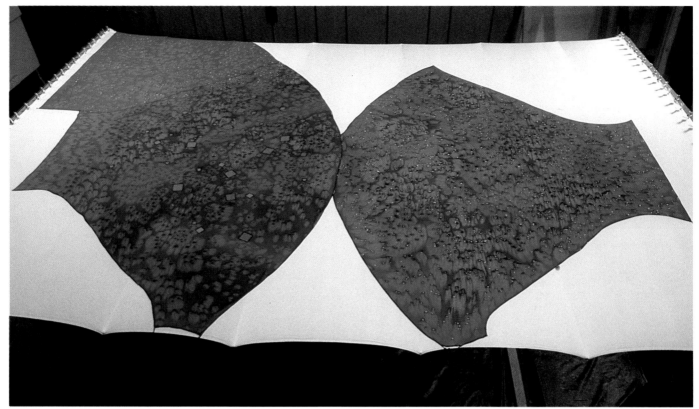

Here you see a large piece of silk crepe de chine being stretched with shinshi and a pair of sawhorses. The outlined blue shapes on the white silk are two very full sleeves for a dress. When you are working with a very large piece of silk, it is often best to use shinshi and harite (see opposite page), or some improvised stretching technique like this one, so that the silk will not sag onto any surface.

DEVICES FOR STRETCHING SILK

You can purchase an adjustable frame, buy canvas stretcher bars, or build a frame. The adjustable frames made specifically for fabric painters can be purchased from mail-order catalogs that service surface designers and craftspeople.

The common canvas stretcher bars can be purchased in most art supply stores. They are sold in pairs and in different lengths, two pairs making a frame. The measurement marked on the stretchers is the outside measurement of the frame, but it is the inside measurement of the frame that will be the size of your finished piece, so buy your stretcher size accordingly.

If your silk-painting projects are large and uniform in size, you can build a frame to your own specifications by using 1 by 2 inch or 2 by 4 inch boards purchased from your local lumberyard. Use metal corner braces to assemble the frame. To avoid problems with large pieces of fabric that may sag onto a tabletop, attach the frame to a pair of sawhorses with four C-clamps, one C-clamp at each corner of the frame. The silk may still sag a little, but it won't touch anything, and you can still paint it.

A traditional Japanese method of stretching fabrics involves the shinshi and the harite. This ingenious support and stretching technique will support small scarves as well as yardage. The shinshi are resilient bamboo rods with needle-sharp points at each end. Shinshi can be purchased through fiber arts mail-order catalogs; see List of Suppliers on page 138. They come in various lengths. The length should be wider than the fabric you are stretching. For example, to stretch a length of silk 45 inches wide, several rods approximately 47½ inches long are positioned across the 45-inch width, and the needle points are inserted into the selvage. The bamboo rods bow, creating the tension needed to keep the fabric stretched. The ends of the fabric are supported by two harite, which are wooden clamps. The bottom of the clamp has needle points to catch and hold the silk; the top of the clamp covers the needle points and clasps the silk into place. The whole system is then secured, hammock style, to anything that will give it support.

If you do not have a harite, you can improvise by using shinshi and 50-inch wooden sawhorses. I have stretched up to three yards of 45-inch-wide fabric by securing the ends to the wooden horses and by using the shinshi to stretch across the width. Because these stretching techniques can be adapted to different lengths and widths of fabrics, the advanced silk painter who is planning to paint many projects of various sizes will find both the shinshi/harite and the shinshi/sawhorses techniques worthwhile alternatives to assembling a frame out of 2 by 4 inch boards for each size project.

DEMONSTRATION:
Stretching Silk with Shinshi and Harite

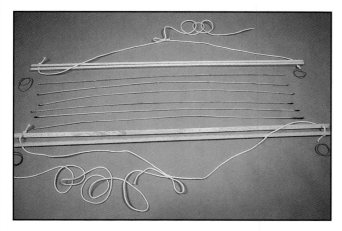

Here are shinshi and homemade harite. To make your own harite, use brass nails (no. 18 ¾-inch brass escutcheon pins), four strips of soft wood (½ by ¾ inch) such as Douglas fir, and pliable rope. The length of the wood strips should be 10 inches (25 cm) longer than the width of the silk; thus a 55-inch harite will accommodate 45-inch fabric.

Sand the wood to eliminate any rough edges that may snag the silk. Now nail the four long strips of wood into two pairs. Hammer the brass nails in a straight line, no more than 1¼ inches apart, through each top strip into the bottom strip. Drill a hole for attaching the rope 1½ inches from each end of the wood strips.

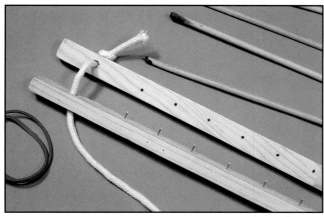

Pry apart the strips of wood that you just nailed together, exposing the needle-sharp points that will catch and hold the silk. With a small drill press and a drill bit slightly larger than the diameter of the nails, enlarge the nail holes so that the two strips of wood will easily fit back together without binding. Attach a rope 1½ times the length of the wood strips to each end. One end of the rope goes through the top hole first; the other end goes through the bottom hole first.

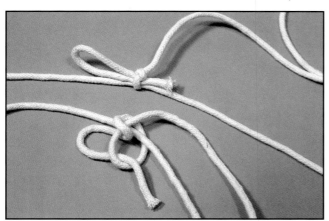

Attach a length of rope to the loop with a handy slip knot as illustrated. The slip knot glides easily so that the level and tautness of the silk can be adjusted.

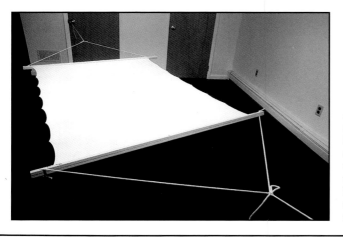

After the fabric is stretched in the harite, tie the hammock-style harite to a support and position the shinshi across the fabric. The shinshi are flexible bamboo rods that arch to stretch the silk taut, so they should be slightly longer than the width of fabric (such as 47½ inches long for fabric 45 inches wide.) In this picture you can't see the shinshi themselves because they are underneath the silk, but they are evident in the "points" along the fabric's edge, where the silk is stretched tightest.

MEASURING AND TEARING THE SILK

When measuring and tearing silk for stretching, consider the inside dimensions of the frame and the measurements of the border you will need for your particular project. Otherwise, measure the length and width of the piece of silk you need, simply hold the edge of your silk up to the inside of the frame and lightly stretch it across, providing a border of ½ to ¾ inch on each side for tacking. Then make a small ¼ to ½ inch cut on the edge of the silk to mark the measurement; do not tear the silk yet. Use the same procedure to mark the perpendicular dimension. Once this is done, you are ready to tear the silk piece free from the yardage.

It is more efficient to tear the amount of silk you want than to cut it. Tearing provides you with a thread-and-grain-perfect piece of silk, which means that you will have a squared piece of silk that has straight sides and right angles. Thread-and-grain-perfect silk will stretch more easily than cut silk, and your design work will not be distorted when the silk is removed from the frame.

Carefully, by applying equal pressure from both hands, tear the silk at the cut measurements. Work back and forth, a few inches at a time, alternating sides of the silk until the two tears meet at right angles and you have freed a thread-and-grain-perfect piece of silk from the yardage.

Most weaves of silk tear easily, but if your silk is too delicate for tearing or you are working with a twill or jacquard weave, you will have to pull threads at each cut measurement until the pull lines meet at right angles. Following the lines created by the pulled threads as a guide, cut your silk piece with a sharp scissor.

DEMONSTRATION: Cutting Silk

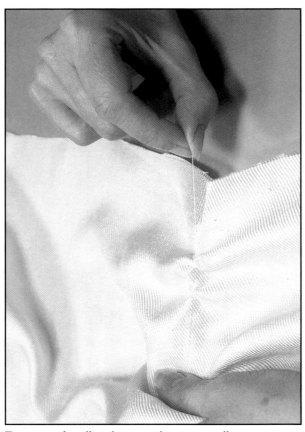

To prepare the silk to be cut with scissors, pull a few threads at each cut measurement until the pull lines meet at a right angle.

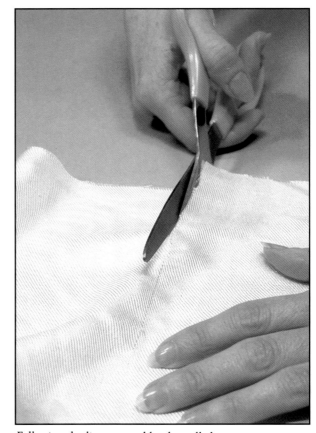

Following the lines created by the pulled threads as a guide, cut the silk with a pair of sharp scissors.

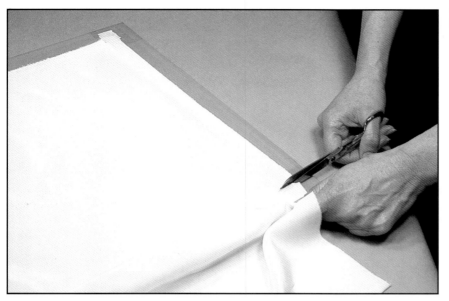

DEMONSTRATION:
Tearing Silk

Hold the edge of the silk up to the frame and lightly stretch it across, providing a border (½ inch (1 cm) for crepe de chine and ¾ inch (2 cm) for weaves with less give) on each side for tacking. Make a small ½-inch (1-cm) cut on the edge of the silk to mark the measurement. Repeat this step for the other side measure.

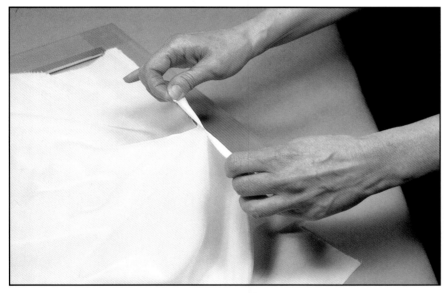

Carefully, by applying equal pressure from both hands, tear the silk at the cut measurements.

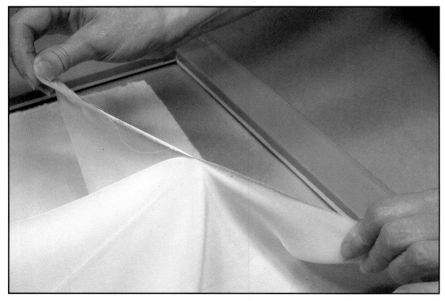

Work back and forth, a few inches at a time on each side of the silk, until the two tears meet at a right angle and you have freed a thread-and-grain-perfect piece of silk from the yardage.

SECURING DEVICES AND STRETCHING TECHNIQUES

There are several devices for securing the silk to the frame. Choosing the right stretching and securing devices for a silk-painting project will make the painting process more efficient and the finished piece more successful. For example, pillows, wall hangings, and paintings need borders for future construction and framing, yardage needs special handling and support, and scarves can look unsightly with tack holes left in finished hems.

Masking Tape

Masking tape is an alternative to tacks and pushpins. If your designs are primarily geometric, stretching your silk with masking tape will help you maintain straight gutta lines. Silk has a memory and will return to its original shape when taken off the frame. Proper stretching, using masking tape, assures that your thread-and-grain-perfect piece of silk is squared in the frame.

Use 1-inch masking tape to secure the silk onto the frame. Masking tape doesn't leave an undesirable gummy residue on the fabric and it holds the silk well when stretched. High humidity and dampness will interfere with the tape's ability to hold onto the silk. If possible, adjust the temperature and humidity in your studio for best results. It takes practice and patience to deal with the sticky masking tape and the stretching. But after taping a few frames of silk, you will become sensitive to how much pull and stretch the tape will withstand.

Tacks and Pushpins

Architects' tacks have three small prongs and are easily pushed into a wooden frame. These tacks lie flat against the frame, so they will not restrict the movement of your drawing arm as you work.

Thumbtacks also lie flat but are more difficult to push into and remove from a wooden frame.

Stainless steel pushpins don't rust and are easily cleaned. If you are doing intricate designs and plan to use pushpins, I suggest you stretch your silk over the frame, securing it on the outside vertical edge of the frame, where the pushpins are out of the way of your drawing hand. When measuring your silk, be sure to add the length of the larger border.

Pushpin.

Thumbtack.

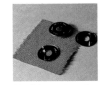

Architects' tacks.

DEMONSTRATION:
Stretching Silk with Masking Tape

Place four strips of 1-inch (2.5-cm) masking tape, sticky side up, on a work surface, and secure the ends with short pieces of tape, sticky side down. Lightly stretch the fabric and lay it down evenly on half the width of the tape.

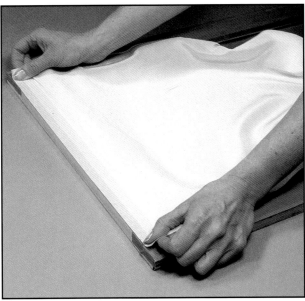

Adhere the silk to the frame by taping the short end first. Keep the tape in a straight line and press it firmly onto the frame. If the tape is not straight, pull it off the frame and try again.

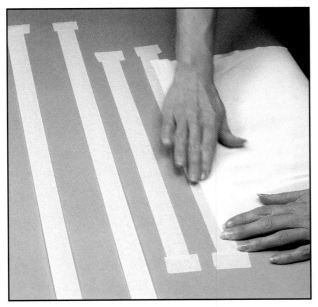

Press firmly.

Release the tape and proceed by applying the opposite side of the fabric to the next strip of tape.

Adhere the adjacent side next, and then the opposite side.

Complete the fourth side by holding onto the taped part of the silk. Then, inch by inch, pull and stretch the silk as you adhere it to the frame. Stretch the silk tightly and maintain a straight line. After completing all four sides, go back and press the tape firmly to the stretcher. For security, overlap another layer of tape, catching ½ inch (1 cm) or less of the silk, and add additional tape to the stretcher.

If a scarf or piece of fabric is shorter than the frame and one side is left hanging free, extend the silk with 1-inch-wide strips of fabric or one long strip of 1-inch fabric. Fasten the short strips to the edge of the silk with straight pins. Then stretch the silk by pulling each strip and tacking the free end of the strip onto the frame. You can also use one long strip by securing it in a zigzag manner.

Silk crepe de chine stretched on canvas stretcher bars secured with pushpins and thumbtacks.

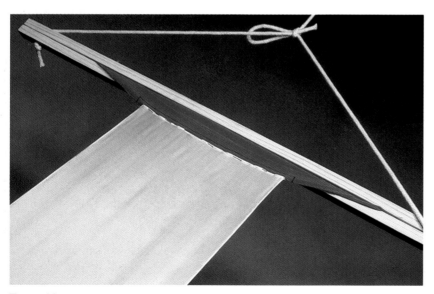

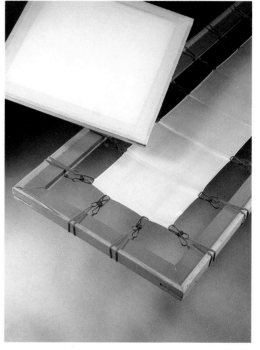

To avoid large pinholes, a scarf with a rolled hem can be extended to stretch on a harite with a piece of fabric and silk pins. To keep the dye from spreading to the harite, apply a heavy resist line on the extension between the scarf and the harite. Fine silk pins through the rolled hem itself will leave very inconspicuous holes later.

Silk stretched on canvas stretcher bars with masking tape provides a more uniformly stretched fabric. This is very important when designs contain straight lines or geometric shapes. Heavy-duty canvas stretcher bars are excellent for stretching scarves with finished hems. Attach with silk clips and rubber bands.

DEMONSTRATION: Stretching Silk with Stretcher Bars and Thumbtacks

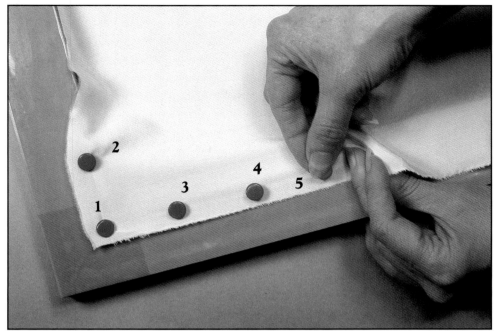

To stretch silk using tacks, put tack **1** in a corner, and then insert tack **2** approximately 2 inches (5 cm) away. Square up the silk with the corner of the frame and get ready to place tack **3** on the other side of tack **1**, the same distance away from tack **1** as tack **2**. Do this by stretching the edge of the silk away from tack **1** with one hand and pushing tack **3** in with the other hand. Continue tacking the silk until you have completed the row. Tack the second row

continuing from tack **2**, being careful to keep the edge of the silk stretched and in a straight line. When you reach the third side (opposite side one), be sure to stretch the silk tautly. When you reach the fourth side, start by placing a tack in the center of the row. Then place a tack in the middle of each half. Continue this process until all the tacks are in place, keeping the border of the silk even and the silk stretched.

Silk Clips and Rubber Bands

Silk clips and rubber bands are great for scarves that have rolled hems. The clips keep the scarf suspended in the frame and free of pinholes, and the rubber bands keep the scarf from sagging during painting.

The size of the frame should accommodate the scarf, the length of the clips, and the rubber bands. For example, a pair of heavy-duty canvas stretcher bars measuring 18 by 63 inches, two dozen clips, plus two dozen rubber bands measuring 7 inches by ⅛ inch will accommodate a scarf that is 9 by 54 inches.

First assemble and tape the frame. Then prepare the clips by slipping one end of the rubber band onto one side of the clip. Stretch the rubber band around the frame and attach the loose end to the other side of the clip.

Before you proceed with stretching the scarf, make sure the clips are spaced evenly and across from each other on the frame. When stretching the scarf, secure opposite sides first, making sure the clips grip the scarf just inside the rolled hem.

When applying color near a clip, momentarily release the pressure of the clip so that the dye will travel under the area where the clip grips the silk. It's all right to reattach the clip while the dye is still wet.

TIPS

• Line the tacking edge of the frame with a washable tape, such as plastic shipping tape, so that you can wipe off any dye with alcohol before you start a new painting. Before applying plastic tape to new stretcher bars, make a surface for the tape to adhere to by roughing up the wood with a coarse piece of sandpaper; then wipe the wood free of sawdust with a damp cloth. Then allow it to dry before applying the tape.

• Remove tacks from a frame by prying them up with a flat-edged tool such as a dull pair of scissors, table knife, or letter opener.

• Make sure tacks and pushpins are free of any dye before reusing them. Drop stained pushpins and tacks into a glass jar containing alcohol and water. Let them soak for a few minutes, then cover and shake the jar to swish off the excess dye. Remove the tacks and lay them out on a few layers of paper towels to dry.

4: PLANNING DESIGNS AND TRANSFERRING THEM ONTO THE SILK

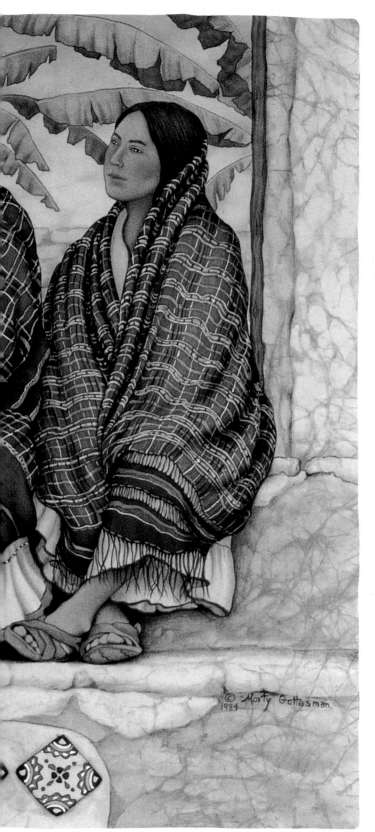

Ladies on the Wall. © *Marty Noble.*

Each artist develops his or her own unique approach to design work, an individual process for creating designs and solving design problems. Because of this, there are a variety of ways to plan designs and transfer them onto a piece of stretched silk.

Some freehand artists draw directly on the silk with gutta, as you have already seen. Others sketch on the silk with pencil and then apply the gutta resist lines, correcting their original drawing. For the rest of us, preplanning a design before transferring it onto the silk gives us the control we need for our design direction. For example, Marty Noble carefully worked out her composition and beautifully drawn details for *Ladies on the Wall* before she began applying her resist.

PREPARING TO APPLY THE RESIST

There are two basic ways to transfer a design: tracing it directly onto the silk with gutta, and tracing it onto the silk with a pencil before applying the resist over the pencil lines.

The following steps and technical considerations apply whichever method you choose.

1. Remember that the inside measurement of the frame will be the size of the finished piece. Before you stretch the silk onto the frame, place the frame on a piece of quality tracing paper. Tracing paper will not absorb gutta. With a pencil, delineate the inside opening of the frame onto the paper. This will be the size of the finished painting, so plan the design within this area.

2. Use a soft pencil when drawing and designing on the tracing paper. If the outline of the design needs to be bolder in order to be visible through the silk, trace over the pencil with a Sharpie permanent marker, which will not bleed when it comes in contact with gutta.

3. Stretch your silk onto the frame (see pages 40–43).

4. When the design on tracing paper is completed, trim the tracing paper to the frame size previously delineated.

5. Slip the design inside the back of the frame. (This is often easiest to accomplish by turning the frame upside down.) The design should be facing up against the back of the silk.

6. To prevent the design from moving or shifting, secure it onto the underside of the frame with tape.

7. Find a book or similar support that will fit within the frame. It should be the same thickness as the frame, or slightly thicker. Cover one side of the support with opaque white paper. This support serves two purposes. It presses the design against the silk so that you can see where to apply the gutta lines, and it acts as a support for your drawing hand. As you apply the gutta, you can move the book around so that it supports whatever section of the design you are working on.

8. Place the support under the frame with the white paper facing up. The support should fit tightly up against the tracing paper so that the design becomes visible through the silk. (If you are continually working with the same size frame, you might consider making a lightweight support that fits snugly inside the frame. To do this, cut three layers of foam-core board to fit inside the frame and tape them together at the sides.)

At this point you should decide whether to trace the design onto the silk with the appropriate pencil or skip this step and apply gutta directly onto the silk. The better method depends partly on the consistency of your resist, so you should test it before making a decision. If you are using gutta, make sure its consistency is on the thick side so that it does not smear between the silk and the tracing paper. (Fresh, unthinned, clear gutta is usually the proper consistency.)

Transferring a preplanned design onto silk with gutta is a very efficient way of working. It eliminates the need to trace your design in pencil onto the silk first. For years my students and I have been applying gutta to the silk with the tracing paper flush to the back of the fabric without any problems with the gutta smearing.

DEMONSTRATION:
Tracing a Pencil Design with Gutta

In preparation for transferring the motif to the silk, stretch the silk on a frame, draw the design clearly on tracing paper, and make a support panel to fit inside the frame.

TRACING A DESIGN IN PENCIL FIRST

If you are using a gutta-like resist, test it to make sure it does not smear when it is applied against the tracing paper and support. If you cannot adjust the consistency of your resist, simply trace your design onto the silk using one of the following pencils. If you are using a clear resist, trace the design with a dressmaker's EZ Washout marking pencil, which is easily removed during the finishing process. (Graphite and charcoal will not always dry-clean or wash out of the silk.) Sharpen the dressmaker's pencil with a razor blade and refine the point with an emery board. If you are using a colored resist, a graphite pencil will do because the lines will be covered by the resist.

Another possibility is a Marvy erasable fabric marker no. 422, whose markings automatically disappear in 2 to 14 days, so be sure to finish applying your gutta before your guidelines disappear. *Caution:* There are several brands of markers and disappearing pens on the market that wash, iron, or fade out of the fabric. The chemicals in these products may react with the gutta and break down the resist. Test them thoroughly on a scrap of silk.

Once you have traced your design with the appropriate pencil, remove the support and tracing from the back of the frame. This will protect your resist from any smearing caused by the tracing paper and support.

You are now ready to apply gutta or a similar resist onto the silk; follow the steps outlined below.

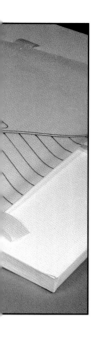

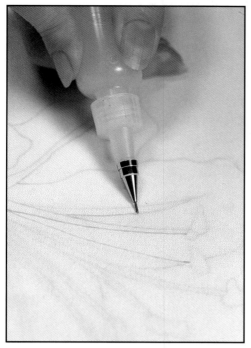

With the tracing taped securely to the underside of the silk and the support panel in place, use the gutta to trace the motif onto the silk.

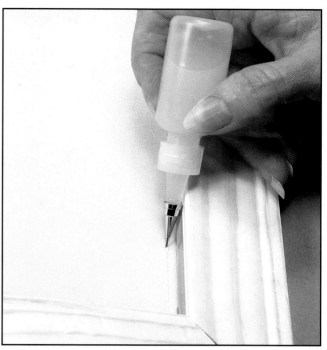

After completely transferring the motif to the silk, remove the support and the tracing paper from the back of the silk, and apply a gutta holding line to the back of the silk around the perimeter of the design. Once the gutta has been applied, do not remove the silk from the frame until you are finished painting it, or the gutta may lose its resist qualities.

TRACING A DESIGN ONTO THE SILK WITH GUTTA OR A SIMILAR RESIST

Whether you are tracing your design directly onto the silk or have already traced it onto the silk with pencil, you will be following almost exactly the same procedure; you will be applying lines of resist that will penetrate the silk and serve as a barrier for liquid dyes.

1. Plan the direction in which you apply the resist so as to avoid smearing already applied resist with your hand.
2. Press the tip of the applicator firmly against the silk so that the resist penetrates it from front to back.
3. Once the gutta has been applied, remove the tracing paper that was previously attached to the underside of the frame. Then wait about 10 minutes for the gutta to dry, and the design is ready to be painted. *Caution:* Never apply dye with the tracing paper attached to the silk! It will absorb and smear the dye.
4. To keep the dye from running onto the frame, apply a gutta line onto the silk around the inside of the frame. Do this on the back of the silk using the inside edge of the frame as a brace and guide for your hand. As you apply the resist, lean the applicator on the frame and place the tip at an angle slightly away from the frame. This will keep your gutta line nice and straight.
5. Check both sides of the silk to see whether all the resist lines have penetrated the silk and are connecting. Make

any necessary resist repairs on the back of the silk to ensure a good thorough seal.
6. Allow the resist enough time to dry. Gutta takes from 10 to 20 minutes to dry completely and may smear if touched when wet. It is not necessary for gutta to be thoroughly dry before you apply the dye; just be careful not to brush up against the resist lines. Most water-based resists should be allowed to dry thoroughly before you apply dye. There are a variety of water-based resists available, each with its own set of properties. Therefore, it is best to test the resist before applying dye. *Caution:* Apply resists only to dry silk, or they will not penetrate the fibers properly.
7. If the painting calls for the layering of colors, you must transfer your design, apply gutta, and paint on the dye in successive steps. Pencil lines may fade, especially when the colors become darker with each application of dye, so the originally traced design may no longer be visible. Therefore, the guidelines for each step of the layering must be delineated before each application of resist and dye.

After the first application of gutta, apply the dye and wait for the silk to dry. Replace the design beneath the stretched silk. To illuminate the back of the design, place the frame over a light table, cover a glass table with a piece of tracing paper and then place a light under the glass, or place the design up against a sunny window. Trace the remaining guidelines with light chalk pencil or an EZ Washout marking pencil.

Surface design © Julie Jennings. This design, like most of Julie's work, was executed freehand. She spontaneously incorporated the ombré technique, described on page 76, with overpainting.

FREEHAND DRAWING WITH GUTTA

If you would like to try a freer approach that does not involve tracing at all, follow these steps:

1. Keep the gutta fluid enough to flow smoothly and easily on the silk. *Caution:* Apply resists only to dry silk without a support under the frame.
2. Press the tip of the applicator firmly against the fabric so that the resist penetrates the silk.
3. Using a full arm motion and without bracing your drawing hand on the frame, lightly squeeze the resist applicator and move in a continuous, smooth motion. Adjust the pressure on the gutta bottle to your particular style. If you move too slowly, the gutta lines will be thick, so squeeze less. If you move too quickly, the gutta lines will be thin, so squeeze more. Be careful not to smear the resist with your hand.
4. Allow the gutta lines to dry 10 to 20 minutes before applying dye.

Some silk painters creatively adapt the technique to their particular painterly approach and free-spirited style by never creating a complete barrier with the resist lines. When they paint, they control and blend the color as it moves in and out of the gutta lines. (For an example, see the surface design on page 13.)

Once your gutta design is in place on the silk and has dried for 10 minutes, you are ready to apply dye. But before you pick up your paintbrush, it is important that you have a basic understanding of how dyes work—how they function as colors on the white silk, how they mix, and how you can use them to blend whatever color you need. The next two sections will explain all this and introduce you to color theory as it applies to dye. You will also learn how to make your own dye color chart, which will prove to be an invaluable tool for mixing (applying and overpainting) dyes on silk. Silk painting is all about beautiful, vibrant color—so read on and discover how to expand your palette as a silk painter.

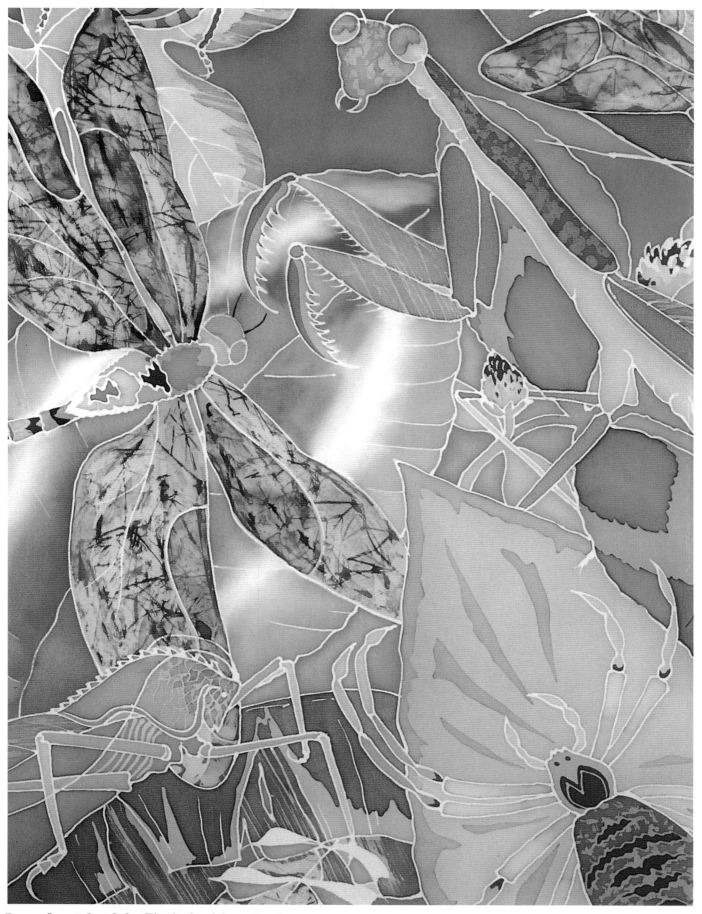

Dragonflies. © *Sissi Siska. This freehand design was drawn primarily in gutta line. Some of the textures were added with wax resist.*

5: SILK AND COLOR

When neon colors became a fashion statement in the 1990s, my friend Seemona showed up on the ski slope wearing a dynamic neon color combination. Her stretch pants were eggplant, a deep, rich red-violet. The dominant color in the print of her jacket was a vivid neon chartreuse. The yellow-green chartreuse and red-violet are near-complementary colors. When complementary colors are placed next to each other they intensify each other. This is what made the color combination of Seemona's ski outfit so eye-catching and dynamic.

Along with the bright chartreuse, the colors in the jacket print included tints of blue and turquoise nestled on a neutral white background. The analogous tints and shades of blue, turquoise, and chartreuse harmonized because of the key color of blue that they all have in common. Seemona's natural strawberry-blond hair topped off her outfit and turned this fashionable color combination into a personal, stunning, and unique color statement. The color of her hair was within the same value range as the blue and turquoise on her jacket, and its hue was also a split-complementary color to the subtle range of blues and greens. This color combination against the snow, highlighted by the sun on the mountain, was a dazzling feast for the eyes.

COLOR THEORY

Color is influenced by many things. Personal preference aside, a particular color is neither beautiful or ugly. How one color works in relationship to other colors, as well as to textures and the space within a design, determines its value and gives it life and presence.

Anyone who wants to work with color can learn to understand why the combination of colors in the ski outfit work together. Creating your own interesting color combinations is a skill that can be developed. To make the process of selecting, mixing, and altering colors easier, you must build a vocabulary to identify the qualities of colors. Understanding the vocabulary of color will enable you to verbalize your perceptions of colors, compare color combinations, constructively criticize your own work, and build a good basic knowledge of color.

Colors are classified by three separate characteristics: hue, value, and intensity. These are known as the three dimensions of color.

Hue is the name of the color, such as yellow-orange, brown, or blue. A hue can be altered by mixing it with another hue to create a new color; for example, by mixing red and yellow, you will create orange.

Value is the lightness or darkness of a color in relation to white and black and has nothing to do with the actual name of the hue. The value of a hue is changed when you add a neutral color—white, black, or gray—to a pure hue.

The value of a hue is described as a tint, tone, or shade. Tints, which are lighter than the pure hue in value, are the hue plus a percentage of white. (For example, pink is a tint of red.) Certain tints are also called pure pastels if they contain a pure hue plus white but no other colors (such as a complement to partially neutralize them). Since silk painters work with transparent color on a white ground, there is no such product as white dye. The silk is the white, so tints are obtained by adding a clear dilutant to the dye, which reduces the concentration of color to be applied to the white silk.

Tones are middle values created in silk painting by combining the hue with gray (black plus dilutant that will bring out the white of the silk). Shades are deeper and darker in value than tones. They are created by adding a few drops of black dye to the pure hue, without adding dilutant.

Intensity, or chroma, is how subtle or bright a color looks. The outer ring of the color wheel contains hues at their most intense. The intensity of a hue can be reduced by adding a touch either of its complementary color or of black; the resulting color will be more neutral and less intense. If you significantly change the intensity of a pure hue like those on the outer ring of the color wheel, you will create earth colors. Complementary colors are directly across from each other on the color wheel: Red complements green, violet complements yellow, yellow complements violet, blue-green complements red-orange, and so on.

Remember that some dyes, like Super Tinfix, come very highly concentrated and actually become *more* vibrant and intense when you dilute them to the concentration intended by the manufacturer before applying them. If you dilute them further, you will create tints.

COLOR HARMONY

The basis of a good color combination is derived from nature. Once you understand the natural laws of harmony you will be able to utilize the concepts to create fresh, interesting color combinations.

Monochromatic color themes are created by using tints, tones, and shades of the same hue. A hue will harmonize with various values and intensities of itself. Therefore, by varying the intensity of a hue, you can create pleasing and successful color combinations often referred to as "harmonies of nuance." For example, pink is a tint, rose is a tone, and maroon is a shade. Because all these colors are made from the same basic red hue, they will haromonize with one another in the same design.

Remember that the artist/colorist knows how to vary the laws of harmony and balance by introducing a disharmonious element. With this in mind, try accenting a monochromatic theme by adding a splash of complementary color to the design.

Analogous colors, which are three to five hues directly next to each other on the color wheel, also work well in combination and are pleasing to the eye. For example, autumn maple trees that range from yellow to red on the color wheel encompass five hues: yellow, yellow-orange, orange, red-orange, and red. These hues used in color combinations are usually interesting as well as successful. You cannot go wrong using analogous colors because they are so closely related. The introduction of one complementary color to an analogous color scheme—such as blue with the autumn maples—creates a split-complementary scheme.

Keep in mind that when analogous colors are placed side by side they intensify each other, but when mixed together they neutralize each other.

Complementary colors and near-complementary colors, which are opposite from each other on the color wheel, are harmonies found in nature. For example, true violets with yellow centers, blue iris with orange centers, and the blue and violet birds of paradise with their yellow and orange contrasts are all striking to the eye.

Color triads are three colors equidistant from each other on the color wheel. These triads used in varying tints, tones, shades, and intensities make dynamic and interesting combinations. There are only four basic combinations: the primary colors (red, yellow, and blue), the secondary colors (orange, violet, and green), and two sets of tertiary colors: yellow-orange, red-violet, and blue-green; and red-orange, blue-violet, and yellow-green.

For drama and strength in a design, one color of the triad should be more dominant and the other two should be used in unequal proportions.

A *dominant hue* is another way to unify a painting. Nature harmonizes colors by mixing them all with a small amount of the same hue. This dominant hue brings all the colors into harmony and creates a mood. For example, a cityscape bathed in the light of a sunset will take on a reddish cast; on a rainy day the landscape will take on a violet to blue-violet cast.

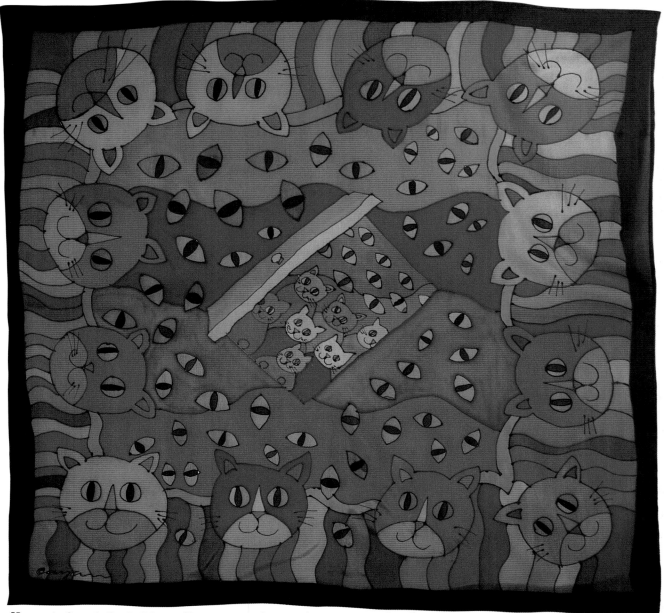

Hypnotic Cats. © Cicely Gilman. Here warm analogous colors are accented with complementary blue and green.

Flowering plants often have a touch of the flower color in their foliage and vice versa. Red poinsettias have red in the stems and leaves, making them a rich deep green. White poinsettias have lighter leaves because there is an absence of red in their foliage.

In silk painting, where colors are mixed by overdyeing (painting one color over another on the silk) or painting over a common background color, the common hue brings all the colors into harmony. The common hue also integrates the colors by slightly neutralizing them and reducing the intensity of the bright, pure hues.

Your colors will be richer and more harmonious once this theory of working with a dominant hue is understood and applied to silk painting.

Random color schemes are useful for drama, excitement, and special effects. This kind of scheme involves risks: It is the most difficult to control because there are no rules. Color decisions are made through a combination of feelings, aesthetic intuition, and experience in color and design. With this in mind, there are a few guidelines and suggestions that you may find useful.

Color and design teach us that any color will work with any other color, given the right proportions and a pleasing variety of shapes and positions in a design. Also, colors can be held together by a dominant factor such as a powerful overall pattern of light or dark. Since white and black hues are neutral and do not have a chroma that will compete with color, they are used to isolate or set off areas of color. For this reason a

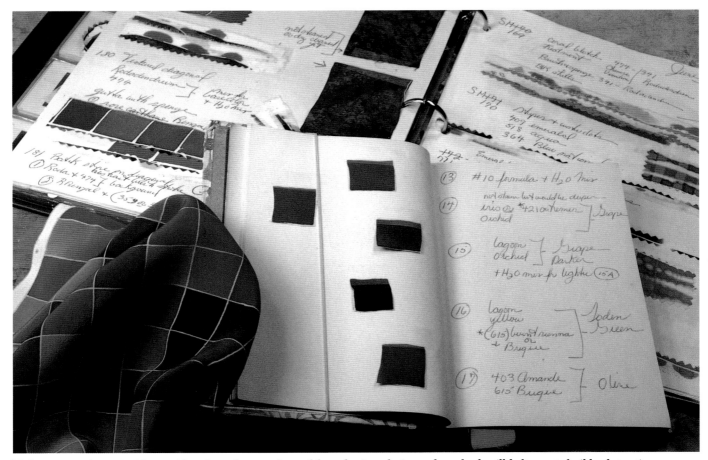

Making notes of your insights and keeping color samples and formulas in a designated notebook will help you to build substantive knowledge about dyes as color. To keep in control of work in progress, keep a piece of silk stretched and handy for testing colors.

dominant light or dark pattern acts as a frame that isolates the color, as well as a design element that holds the colors together. For example, colors that are placed between the black squares of a checkerboard pattern are isolated by the black and held together by the checkerboard design. Random colors can also be set off by placing them on a white and/or black background.

A *word of caution:* When you are working in a random color scheme, don't let a creative high carry you away. If you hesitate and become indecisive about what to do next, stop! Chances are the scheme will be complete. If not, now may be the time to refer to your library of colors for visual support and reference. You may also need to strengthen a dominant factor, add variety to the proportions of your colors, or adjust the placement of your colors.

To be successful with a random color scheme, an artist must have an intuitive sense of beauty plus a keen sense of proportion and balance for both color and design. To improve these artistic judgments, learn from your successes and mistakes.

The Subtractive Primaries
When working with dyes and reflective materials such as silk, the subtractive primaries are used to mix all the colors. The three subtractive primaries (also known as process colors) are the most important: clear yellow, turquoise (cyan) and fuchsia (magenta). In subtractive color mixing, which applies to dyes, the colors subtract (or absorb) parts of the full spectrum of

light and reflect back to our eyes the remaining parts of the spectrum, which we see as color.

In theory the three subtractive primaries are the only hues necessary for color mixing. But I have found it easier and more expedient to mix a range of colors by also stocking orange, red-orange, a reflex blue (a deep blue-violet), blue-green, warm brown, cool brown, and black.

Theoretically, black can be achieved by mixing equal amounts of the primaries. But in reality, the purity and strength of the pigment is contaminated by the extenders and bases used to make the dye, so that it is difficult to mix a really rich black. (The same is true with paint, pastels, colored pencils, and so on.)

The two browns are used to mix earth tones. Combinations of the nine colors plus black will produce an infinite number of colors.

Even though you can mix all your colors from the nine basic hues plus black, you may discover a need for large quantities of a particular hue. You may also find certain colors, such as vivid violet or a true red, difficult to mix. It may become economical and convenient for you to expand your stock of dyes by buying a few more premixed hues from the wide range offered by H. Dupont, Sennelier, and other French dye manufacturers.

As mentioned earlier, colors are not always consistent from one bottle of dye to the next. Therefore, mix all the color you need before you begin a project.

MIXING DYE COLORS

There are two approaches to color mixing when you are working with dyes (transparent colors). Either premix the color and apply it to the white silk, or create colors by overdyeing. (Silk painters refer to the overdyeing process as overpainting or layering colors.) Overdyeing eliminates white resist lines and allows you to build up colors and images gradually. In either case the general rules of color mixing are the same. When premixing or overdyeing, combine up to three hues (or procedures) to make a new color. In most cases a fourth will produce a muddy color.

To understand how to alter colors and the effects of each procedure, try this simple exercise.

To mix a color analyze the color you are duplicating by hue (procedure 1), intensity (procedure 2), and value (procedure 3).

1. To mix a hue:

Start with the hue that is closest to the color you plan to achieve. If you need to mix this hue, combine only two colors from the color wheel to produce it. For example, mix two primaries to get a secondary.

primary plus primary = secondary

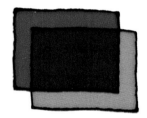

Mix magenta with cyan
or
Overpaint magenta with cyan
to get
violet

2. To alter the intensity of a hue:

Add a touch of the complementary color to produce an earth color. For example, to achieve a less intense violet, add a touch of yellow. (Earth colors can also be achieved by adding brown, as illustrated by the color layering chart.)

hue plus a touch of its complement = less intense hue

Mix violet with a touch of yellow
or
Overpaint violet with a tint of yellow
to get a
less intense violet

3. To alter the value of a hue *(to create a tint, tone, or shade):*

Add white (dilutant) to make a tint; gray (dilutant plus black) to make a tone; or a touch of black or the complementary color to make a shade.

a. hue plus white = tint

Mix violet with dilutant
to get a
tint of violet

b. tint plus black = tone

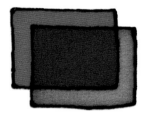

Mix a tint of violet with a touch
of black
or
Overpaint a violet tint with a light gray
to get a
tone of violet

c. hue plus black = shade

Mix violet with a touch of black
or
Overpaint violet with a light gray
to get a
shade of violet

TIPS

• In a monochromatic color scheme, the hue is altered only slightly. Therefore, several layers of different tints, tones, and shades can be overdyed on the silk without creating muddy colors.

• When you are overdyeing, best results are achieved by first applying the purest and lightest hue to the surface and progressing to the deepest and darkest. Remember to limit the layers of concentrated hues to two or three applications, because adding a fourth hue will muddy your color.

6: THE PROCEDURE FOR APPLYING DYE

Understanding the behavior of silk dyes helps you get control over your medium and develop your own artistic style. The color chart project in this section will help you develop this control while simultaneously teaching you about the interaction of colors to broaden your palette.

When several of my fellow silk painters were being introduced to silk painting, they found my color chart project very helpful. They suggested that this chart be the hands-on focus for this book.

Through the process of drawing and painting the chart, you will become familiar with the basic materials, procedures, and skills of silk painting without the added pressure of trying to create a unique design. Like my students, you will also grow to appreciate your finished chart as you repeatedly refer to it when making subsequent color and design decisions.

Surface design © Julie Jennings.

MAKING YOUR OWN DYE COLOR CHART

The color chart project in this section (see pages 62–63) is made up of four separate components: the color wheel clock; the color layering chart; tints, tones, and shades; and gray values. I have combined the chart into a handy exercise that will enable you to control and understand dyes as color.

The Color Wheel Clock

I was introduced to color theory by a very gifted teacher and artist, Barbara Carr. She teaches with insights that come from her experience both with color and the learning process. Out of this experience Barbara developed the color wheel clock. This clock is a very familiar memory tool for understanding and using the color wheel and a handy system for setting up and maintaining a palette of colors.

Color Layering Chart

Joan Berglund is one of my students. As she advanced in her ability, she began to layer one color over another (a process also called overdyeing or overpainting). The need to understand how colors are achieved and altered by the process silk painters call layering motivated Joan to paint an extensive reference chart of colors. Joan is now quite an experienced silk painter, but still she never works without her color chart handy. I have included a simplified version of this valued reference chart as the main element of this project.

Tints, Tones, and Shades

I traditionally gave beginning students an exercise in altering colors to make tints, tones, and shades. Through this project they became familiar with mixing tints by adding the dilutant, shades by adding black, and tones by adding the dilutant plus black.

Gray Values

Since the concentration level of dyes varies from bottle to bottle and company to company, it is impossible to determine a formula for a true value scale. Therefore, it is very helpful to practice diluting your black to create your own reference for a range of grays.

SUPPLIES AND MATERIALS

Decide on the type of dyes you plan to use (either French or Jacquard, but not both for the same project because they are formulated differently). Then purchase the colors required to mix the fifteen colors listed on the dye chart guide found on page 61.

Note: In order to introduce novice silk painters to their products, a few of the suppliers who import the French dyes (H. Dupont and Tinfix) are packaging dye kits. Each kit contains approximately 1 ounce (30 ml) of each of the basic colors for mixing. Jacquard dyes can be ordered by color in 2-ounce (59-ml) bottles. If you order a kit, ask what colors and accessories the kit includes. The names of the French dyes may not correspond exactly with the colors I have suggested, but if the kit includes the subtractive primaries and the secondaries plus black and a brown, you will be able to mix the intermediate colors. It has been my experience that

these kits, if used wisely, contain enough dye to complete a dye chart, to experiment further with the behavior of the dyes and specific techniques (shading, salt, alcohol, and so on), and to do a silk painting. You will also need:

Two sets of canvas stretcher bars to make a frame 16 by 22 inches (41 by 56 cm)

1-inch (2½-cm) masking tape

Pencil

Straightedge or ruler

Heavy-weight tracing paper

Support to fit inside frame. (See photo on facing page.)

Scissors

A piece of pure white silk: pongee, heavy-weight China silk, or crepe de chine, measuring approximately 14 by 22 inches (36 by 56 cm), plus scraps for testing your colors and gutta

A tray large enough to hold the dyes, brushes, water, and so on. (The tray keeps your palette organized, contains any accidental spills, and makes clean-up more efficient.) See photo on page 60.

Dropper

Squeeze bottle for dilutant

Dilutant. (I used H. Dupont dye thinner.)

Clear gutta. (Those experienced with gutta may use black dry-cleanable gutta.)

Gutta applicator: size 5 for clear gutta, size 3 for black gutta

Gutta thinner: H. Dupont, Sennelier, or Turpenoid. (The gutta needs to be thick for this project, so you may not need to add any thinner or Turpenoid.)

Fifteen containers for color palette. Small weighted glass cups do not tip as easily as plastic cups. (Since dyes evaporate quickly and you will be working with small quantities, the containers need to be small so that a minimum of dye surface is exposed to the air.)

Six or more small containers with lids for storing mixed colors.

Measuring spoons (stainless steel or plastic): ⅛ teaspoon (.6 ml), ¼ teaspoon (1.2 ml), ½ teaspoon (2.5 ml), 1 teaspoon (5 ml), and 1 tablespoon (15 ml). If you don't have a ⅛ teaspoon measure, count out half the number of drops it takes to fill the ¼ teaspoon.

At least one watercolor round. A Prolene brush would work well for this project because it is easily cleaned and will not flood the small rectangles with too much dye.

Brush holder with clean water.

Absorbent paper towels

Cotton swabs

Rubber gloves for mixing dyes and for clean-up

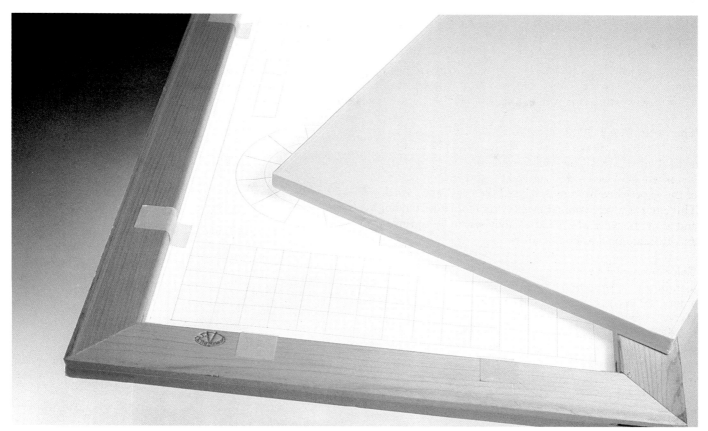

Draw the color chart layout on tracing paper. Tape it to the back of the silk and the back of the frame, and insert the foam-core support in the frame.

PROCEDURE

1. Assemble the frame.
2. Draw the inside shape of the frame on the tracing paper.
3. Cut out the inside shape from the tracing paper.
4. With a ruler and pencil, draw the chart on pages 62–63 onto the tracing paper.
5. Stretch the silk onto the frame using the masking tape technique described on pages 40–41.
6. Tape the color chart guide to the back of the silk and frame so that the tracing paper is next to the silk.
7. Place the frame over the support.
8. Fill the gutta applicator three-quarters full with gutta.
9. Test the gutta on a scrap of silk. The consistency of the gutta should be thin enough to penetrate the silk but still thick enough so that after it has been applied, the lines do not widen or smudge between the tracing and the silk. Most of the time fresh gutta is the proper consistency. (If the gutta is thin and you do not want to wait for it to air-thicken, lightly trace the chart onto the silk with a pencil and ruler. Then remove the support and tracing paper.)
10. Trace the chart onto the silk with gutta.
11. When you have finished applying the gutta, remove the support and tracing from the back of the silk.
    Caution: Never apply dye to the silk with the paper and support in place.
12. Check the back of the silk and repair any gutta lines that are not connected or penetrating the silk.

Trace the chart onto the silk in black dry-cleanable gutta, pressing the applicator up against the silk as you trace along the guidelines. You must continually be aware of the quality of the linear barrier as a resist. Therefore, before you progress too far, check the back of the silk. Are the gutta lines penetrating and sealing the fabric? Are all the stops and starts connected, making a complete linear barrier? If not, you may need to adjust the pressure and speed of your application so that the gutta penetrates the fabric. This is not an exercise in perfection, so don't be concerned if your gutta lines are shaky. Consistent, smooth lines come with practice.

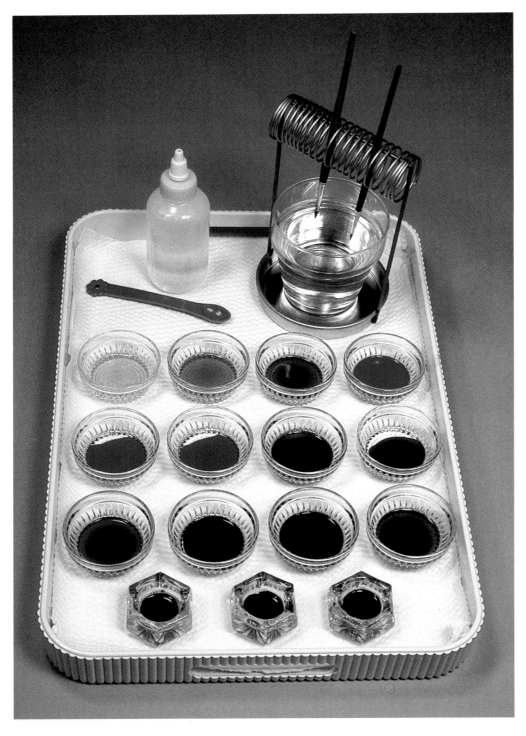

On this tray you see the fifteen key colors, arranged in the order that they will be used to paint the color chart. The tray also holds a brush holder, containers of water and dilutant, and a measuring spoon.

Hue and Its Number on Color Wheel Clock	French Dyes (Can be mixed with each other)		Jacquard Silk Colors (Should not be mixed with French dyes; formulated differently)
	Super Tinfix, Tinfix	H. Dupont	
12. Yellow *	Bergamote yellow	Canari 393	Yellow 703
1. Yellow-orange	12 + a few drops of 2	Madrilene 406	5 parts 703 + 1 part 706
2. Orange	Clementine	Camélia 474	Apricot 706
3. Red-orange/red	Orient red	1 + 4†	Scarlet 712
4. Fuchsia *	Orchid	Cerisette 390	Magenta 714
5. Red-violet	4 + 6†	Fuchsia 353	Digital 717
6. Violet	4 + 8†	4 + 8†	Purple 718
7. Blue-violet	6 + 8†	6 + 8†	Royal blue 722
8. Blue *	Blue lagoon	Blue roy 108 or Ara 518	Cyan 725 or Turquoise 730
9. Blue-green	8 + a few drops of 12	Émeraude 409	1 part 703 + 1 part 730
10. Green	12 + 8†	12 + 8†	Kelly Green 735
11. Yellow-green	12 + a few drops of 8	12 + a few drops of 8	10 parts 703 plus 1 part 730
13. Warm brown	Red brown	Condor 358	Brown siena 745
14. Cool brown	Tobacco	Loutre 342	Chocolate brown 750
15. Black	Ebony black	Noir 700N	Black 759

* Primary color   †Mix one part of each color

SETTING UP THE PALETTE

1. You will need approximately 1 teaspoon (5 ml) of the fifteen colors listed. Tape a scrap of silk to the side of your work table for testing your colors. Use the dye chart mixing guide above to mix the twelve colors of the color wheel clock. Remember, different brands of French dyes can be mixed with one another, but they should not be mixed with Jacquard dyes. Also, because of the variation in dyes and printing, your colors may vary slightly from those on the chart. Store the amount of each color you needed to mix (1 teaspoon, or 5 ml) in a small tightly capped container.

2. Prepare the tray with a layer of paper towels and the fifteen glass saucers, ⅛ teaspoon (.6 ml), brush, brush holder, water, and dilutant.

3. Place ⅛ teaspoon (.6 ml) of each color plus two drops of dilutant in the glass saucers. Wash and dry the spoon between colors. Using the color chart as guide, keep the colors in sequence by starting with yellow (color 12), yellow-orange (color 1), orange (color 2), and so forth.

On the next two pages is the dye color chart. Detailed instructions for executing it follow, through page 67. Completing the various sections of the chart will give you a good understanding of how dyes function as color. The finished chart will also be an invaluable reference for you later.

PAINTING THE KEY COLORS

Before you touch a brushful of dye to the silk, the following do's and don'ts will help you apply the dye effectively. Part of the technique of painting on silk is to let the flow of the dye do the work for you. Therefore, apply the dye slightly inside the gutta line and let the dye travel up to the resist. If you place your brush too close to the gutta line it may slip onto the line and stain the gutta—or worse, the dye may spread into another rectangle.

Since the rectangles are small and require only a little dye, be careful not to create puddles of dye by overloading your brush. Although you may need only one stroke of the brush to fill a space, to avoid streaking and to ensure an even application of dye, overlap any subsequent brushstrokes and try to apply the same quantity of dye to each space.

For easy access to your dyes you may want to keep the container of dye in your hand or within easy reach of your brush. Just be careful not to place it where it can be bumped and spilled! Also, keep the ferrule of your brush free of dye or water so it doesn't drip as you carry it across the silk.

Now you are ready to paint your color layering chart and color wheel clock. This is not an exercise in making a perfect chart but rather an adventure that will help you discover how to work with dyes as color. Each color has a unique behavior. This is true in any medium. Some colors are more concentrated, some mix better than others, some layer without streaking and some don't. This exercise will help you understand the nature and characteristics of your medium.

Apply each key color to its proper place in the layering chart and the color wheel clock. (See steps 1 through 7 under "Painting the Key Colors" on this page.)

1. The layering chart is shaped like a flight of stairs. Start with the top row, in the third vertical column from the left, which will be your column of key colors. (You'll fill in the first two columns later.) Starting from this column, you will paint one color at a time horizontally across the chart. Paint yellow (color 12) at the top of the column.
2. Also paint yellow in the next rectangle to the right. As you fill in the first layer of the chart, there will be two yellow rectangles, three yellow-orange ones, four orange ones, and so on.
3. Paint the yellow in the twelve o'clock wedge on the outer ring of the color wheel chart. (Now you understand why yellow is color 12: It corresponds to twelve o'clock. You may remember this more easily by thinking of a sunny high noon.)
4. Thoroughly wash your brush, and blot the brush and ferrule on a paper towel before changing to the next color.
5. Proceed with yellow-orange (color 1). Paint it in the key color column under the yellow, the two squares to the right that make up the row of yellow-orange, and the outer one o'clock wedge of the color wheel clock.
6. Proceed as above with each color until you have painted all 12 colors on the chart and each color in its time and place in the outside ring of the color wheel clock.
7. Paint colors 13 and 14 (the warm and cool browns) across the bottom two rows of the layering chart.

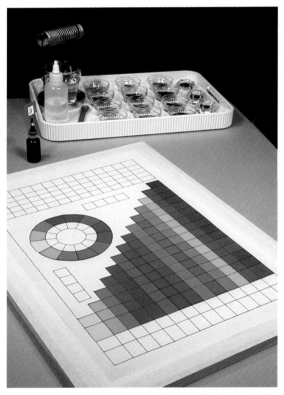

This photo shows the layering chart and color wheel clock after all the key colors have been applied. The bottom rows of the layering chart show the browns, which do not appear on the clock.

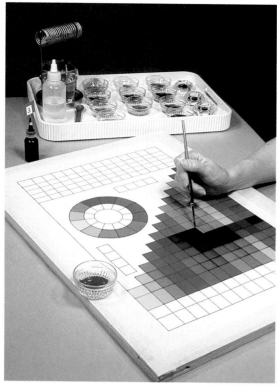

Now overpaint the layering chart, working vertically in columns. Remember not to overpaint the third column from the left, which will show the key colors. (See steps 8 through 10 under "Painting the Key Colors" on this page.)

Keep your gutta bottle handy for quick touch-ups in case the dye seeps out through a break where the gutta did not seal the silk completely. For more on correcting mistakes, see pages 80–81.

Note: After the silk dries, you may notice that a few squares in a row of color may be slightly darker. This is due to more liquid dye being applied in some squares than others. Don't consider this a flaw, but to help eliminate it in the future, don't overload your brush with dye.

8. After the silk is dry, add a second layer of dye to the layering chart. This time, apply each color vertically in a column. Once again start with yellow (color 12), but in the *fourth* column from the left. Layer the yellow down the entire column, over the colors that are already there. (The top "stairstep" of each column will have two layers of the same color.) *Caution:* Do not apply any dye over the third column from the left, which is your column of key colors, dyed only once.

9. Next layer the yellow-orange (color 1) down the column that starts with yellow-orange.

10. Continue with all the colors until all the colors have been cross-layered. The two columns at the far left will still be blank; you will fill them in later. *Save the dyes.*

Adding Earth Tones to the Color Wheel Clock

The colors that remain from executing the layering chart are used to mix the inner earth tone circle on the color wheel clock.

1. Start with yellow and add one drop of complementary (which is violet, color 6). The complementary colors are found directly across from each other on the color wheel.

2. Mix the color well with your brush and apply it in the space under the yellow.

3. Continue by adding one or two drops of each color's complement to each of the twelve hues in the color wheel until you have completed the inner circle.

4. Clean your brushes and other supplies.

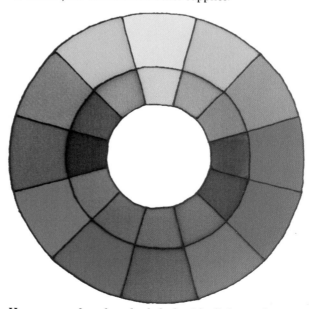

Here you see the color wheel clock with all the earth tones applied to its inner ring, as described in steps 1 through 4 above.

PAINTING TINTS

Tints are a hue plus white. When you are working with liquid dyes on white silk, tints are a hue plus dilutant. Executing a tint chart will help you discover the concentration level of each color and the subtle range of tints that can be achieved by adding a dilutant.

1. Set up your tray with a container of fresh water, a brush, a glass dish, measuring spoons, and paper towels. Keep the containers of the 14 key colors and clean dishes handy.
2. Pour ⅛ teaspoon (.6 ml) of yellow dye plus two drops of dilutant into a glass container. Mix with your brush and paint the first rectangle.
3. Add ⅛ teaspoon (.6 ml) of dilutant to the container of dye. After each addition of dilutant, thoroughly mix the tints with your brush. Using the chart as a guide, paint the tint in the second rectangle of the horizontal row.
4. Add ¼ teaspoon (1.2 ml) of dilutant to the previous mixture, stir, and paint the third rectangle.
5. Add ½ teaspoon (2.5 ml) of dilutant, stir, and paint the fourth rectangle.
6. Add 1 teaspoon (5 ml) of dilutant, stir, and paint the fifth rectangle.
7. Continue in the color clock sequence: 12, 1–11, and finally the two browns (13 and 14). You can save the tints for a future project or discard them.

Now you are ready to dilute hues to make tints. This tray contains a container of water, a bottle of H. Dupont dilutant, plastic measuring spoons, two watercolor rounds in a brush holder, and a glass container of dye. As with all silk-painting projects, organize all your materials before you start, and keep them on a tray to contain any spills.

Squeeze the dilutant into the correct measuring spoon and add it to the dye.

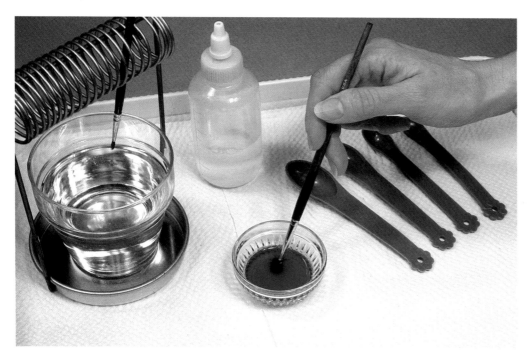

Apply the tint to the correct rectangle of the tint chart.

Then stir with the brush to mix the dilutant and dye thoroughly.

PAINTING SHADES AND TONES

Shades are the hue plus black. Now it is time to paint shades into the second column of the layering chart, just to the left of the key colors. The liquid measurement for the 14 shades is ⅛ teaspoon (.6 ml) of each color of dye plus one or two drops of black. *Save the shades* to make tones.

Tones are the hue plus black and white. Add ⅛ teaspoon (.6 ml) of dilutant to the 14 shades you just completed and paint them in the first column of the layering chart, to the left of the shades. You may now save the dyes for a future project or discard them.

This is the far left section of the layering chart. From left to right, it shows tones, shades, and key colors. Shades are the key color plus black. Tones are the key color plus black and dilutant.

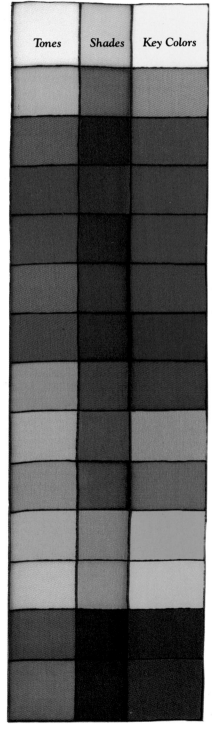

Tones	Shades	Key Colors

Mixing Grays

You will have to determine a formula for diluting black according to the concentration of your black dye. Starting with the same formula you used for tints, run a test on a scrap piece of silk. If necessary, adjust the amount of dilutant you add before applying the formula to your color chart. Two coats of dye are needed to achieve a rich black.

The Finished Chart

Steam-set the dyes by following the steaming instructions on pages 134–137. Keep the chart out of direct sunlight. Since you will frequently refer to your chart while in the midst of a project, protect it from accidental stains by placing it between two sheets of clear plastic.

TIPS

• By selecting two blue primaries for color mixing, you will be able to control the degree and intensity of the secondary mixtures with much more accuracy. For example, the Jacquard turquoise 730 and yellow 703 will produce a variety of relatively intense greens. The cyan 725 and yellow 703 will produce less intense greens because the cyan has a touch of red in it, which alters (grays down) the intensity of the green.

• When you are using the French dyes, a reflex blue such as H. Dupont blue national 362 or a blue-violet such as blue national 364 combined with Super Tinfix orchid or H. Dupont cerisette 390 will help you achieve a beautiful intense range of blues to blue-violets.

• Since the subtractive primaries used to mix dyes are the same as those used to mix commercial printing inks (when you substitute dilutant for white), the PANTONE®* Color Formula Guide used by graphic designers can be a valuable reference for mixing color. The guide can be purchased at professional art supply stores that serve graphic designers.

Pantone, Inc., has very high standards for color reproduction. These standards cannot be met here because color reproduction varies when working with dye, photography, and printing. Therefore, I cannot give you any cross-references to specific colors. But if you have the subtractive primaries plus the orange, red, and blue-green listed on page 61, plus a reflex blue such as H. Dupont blue national 362, you will be able to use the guide for color mixing.

*Pantone, Inc.'s check-standard trademark for color.

SHADING AND BLENDING

One of the many inspirational experiences I have had while putting this book together was two and a half days of collaboration with fellow silk painter Julie Jennings. Out of this exchange came an understanding of several different approaches to the shading and blending of color to create the illusion of form.

When shading a leaf, petal, seashell, and so on, Julie starts by drawing the outline of the shapes with a gutta line. Then she applies a solution of 1 part alcohol and 1 part water inside the area she is planning to shade. After the dilutant has dried just enough so that it doesn't puddle, she starts blending and shading her colors on the wet silk. Because the silk is saturated with the alcohol and water, any color applied to it will not spread as quickly as when dye is painted directly onto dry silk. Also, the dye dries more slowly, providing Julie with the time to control the placing and blending of colors. Sometimes the effect is very bold and painterly. Other times Julie achieves a very soft and sensitive rendered effect, depending upon how much time she spends blending and adding color, and the wetness of the silk.

Unlike Julie, who blends and shades on wet silk, I often blend and graduate colors on dry silk. It helps to remember a few things. For example, dry silk soaks up more color than wet silk. When you are working with a strong color, the result can range from very deep and rich to bright and luminous. If you choose a diluted color, the result will be very soft and pastel. To avoid ridges of dye and streaking, always overlap your brushstrokes. The dye will dry faster on dry silk than on wet silk, so plan ahead and work quickly. Finally, when you are blending and shading, especially within small motifs, a little dye goes a long way.

As long as the silk is still damp, you can continue to manipulate the dye with alcohol. With practice, you will be able to use the alcohol to draw, shade, and highlight a petal into a beautiful dramatic form. Working with alcohol or dye on dry, painted silk is another alternative to creating form, texture, and interest in a design. To understand how to control this technique, see pages 110–111.

Julie Jennings has a very practical use for the little dried-out cups of dye that gather in most silk painters' studios. She uses the concentrated dye to add accents to her flowers and leaves. First, she lets the silk painting dry thoroughly. Then she dips a semidry brush into the concentrated dye. After she tests the dye and is sure it is of a consistency that won't travel on the silk, she paints in the dry-brush accents.

Once you have tried the shading and blending techniques demonstrated here, you will have the basic foundation needed to create the illusion of form in your designs. As your skills improve, you will intuitively add to your fundamental skills, and a personal style will evolve, reflecting the individual way you shade and control the dye to create form.

Hawaii. © Julie Jennings. In this richly shaded tropical design, Julie was able to achieve a different shaded effect for each type of flower. She worked on a wet ground.

Diagonal Feathers. © *Sissi Siska. A light, delicate feeling was achieved in this surface design of beautifully drawn feathers, carefully shaded.*

Primary Hibiscus. © *Julie Jennings. Here Julie was able to add interest to her design elements and primary coloration by shading the flowers and leaves. The shading and drawing give the motifs the form that brings them into the foreground.*

Garden Flowers. © *Julie Jennings. This floral design was inspired by the few days that Julie and I spent exchanging ideas and techniques. Most of the flowers were shaded using Julie's method of working on a wet ground. The leaves were shaded by applying the dye and blending the color on dry silk.*

Rubrum Bamboo. © Susan L. Moyer. By using alcohol dilutant only on the areas where the motif would go, I was able to shade the lily on a wet ground and blend the color of the bamboo leaves on a dry ground.

Lilies on Red, detail. © Susan L. Moyer. This swimwear design contrasts the delicately shaded form of the purple lily against a red blotch background.

Flowers and Fans. © Susan L. Moyer. The flowers in this home furnishings design were shaded using the technique demonstrated in this section. The textures around the pond lily and the drop of water on the lily pad were created by using salt and alcohol techniques covered later in this book.

DEMONSTRATION: Shading and Blending to Create Form

To shade the petals of a flower from a deep color at the center to a light and lacy edge, set up six small cups on a tray. The first three cups will contain different strengths of dye. The dye in the first cup is full strength, with the addition of one or two drops of dilutant to help it flow. In the second cup, add enough dilutant to the dye to make a medium tint. The third cup of dye is diluted to a very light tint, and the fourth cup is filled with dilutant (7 parts alcohol to 3 parts water). In the fifth cup, place a few drops of a deep color that will give you depth for shading. The last cup contains a few drops of a bright color that you can use for highlights. You can set up your dyes exactly like this or slightly differently, according to your own project.

To create a lacy white edge on the petals, brush a small amount of the dilutant around the lower edge of the petal. This small amount of dilutant holds the dye back from penetrating the area you want to keep light. As you paint, periodically refresh this "hold" with a touch more of the dilutant.

Now that you are ready to add color, use a small watercolor round or squirrel-hair quill brush as demonstrated. Start at the base of the petal and apply the darkest color first. A little of this concentrated color will go a long way. As long as the silk is wet, more dye can be added later, so start with a light touch.

Quickly rinse and blot your brush and apply the premixed medium tint, and then the light tint, overlapping the brushstrokes and blending the tints as you work.

(Continued on next page)

(Continued from preceding page)

Carefully, with a clean brush, blend the lightest tint into the white edge of the petal where the dilutant was applied.

If too much color is seeping into the white, apply a little more dilutant to the edge. You will see the dye being pushed back by the dilutant to leave a white edge. You may need to control this reaction by picking up the excess dilutant or dye with a cotton swab.

While the silk is still wet but without puddles, add the accent colors that you have already set up. To create form in the petal, use a small watercolor round brush to apply a touch of the deep shade at the edge of the petal, along the vein, and at the base of the petal.

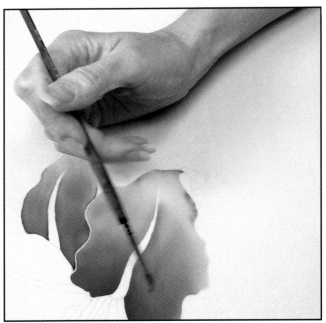

To add highlights in the areas where the form catches the light, use a watercolor round and blend in a touch of the highlight color. To ensure a smooth blending, apply the new color while the silk is wet.

To create shading and depth, add a touch of the complementary color. For example, at the base of this petal I am adding a touch of the petal's red to the green strip down the center. This will reduce the intensity of the green vein and give the petal form.

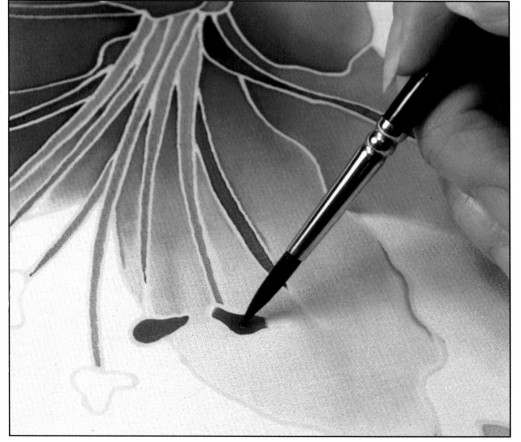

When painting areas that need only a touch of color, work with a watercolor round. Since the squirrel-hair quill brushes hold a lot of dye, they tend to let go of too much, causing small areas to flood with color or the dye to run over the gutta resist barrier.

PAINTING BACKGROUNDS

There are basically two methods for applying color to large areas such as backgrounds. One is called a blotch, which is a color applied to white silk around a painted motif. The other is called a ground, which is a color applied as an underpainting for overdyeing and layering images. The method you choose will be determined by the desired outcome and by the color relationships you are using.

Flat wash, graded wash, ombré, or a random combination of colors that blend together are a variety of effective grounds that can be achieved. A ground color is usually painted first before the resist is applied and then either the background or the motif is overdyed to bring out the image.

Although layering of images and overdyeing will integrate a design and eliminate white gutta lines, the ground color may neutralize the successive applications of color, limiting the artist's ability to produce contrasting or intense hues. For example, if your ground is yellow, you can achieve a bright green by overdyeing with blue, but you cannot achieve a bright violet because yellow and violet are complementaries that will neutralize each other when mixed together. Therefore, if you are working with contrasting hues, such as a split-complementary color scheme, at least one of the complementary hues must be applied to the white silk before the blotch color is applied, even if that blotch color will serve as a ground when you overdye other areas of the painting. For example, to paint a hot pink flower with blue, blue-green, and green foliage and background, first outline the flower motif in gutta and paint the image with hot pink dye. Next proceed by painting a blue blotch around the flower. This blotch becomes a ground in the final stages of the painting, when you overdye the blue with shades of green and yellow to create the foliage and background images.

The other way to achieve contrasting and intense hues in a motif or background is by painting a blotch on white silk around a motif to which gutta has already been applied. In either case, speed, low surrounding temperatures, and the proper brushes are the keys to success when painting large areas.

To facilitate speed, prepare all the dyes in quantities needed for your entire background. Organize your brushes and other equipment before you begin.

When painting a ground color, be sure the silk is stretched tightly on the frame since wet fabric will sag, especially crepe de chine. To contain the liquid dye on the stretched silk, draw a gutta line around the inside edge of the frame. If the painting is very large, place a prop, such as a block of wood, under each corner of the frame to raise the silk and keep it from sagging onto the work surface. (Ideally, all four corners should be propped up to the same height.) Work on a flat surface with a large foam brush or a cotton ball held by a clothespin. Apply the dye across the silk quickly and evenly from side to side. To ensure even application, overlap the strokes slightly. If possible, use a brush that will hold enough dye so that you can start and finish every stroke at the edge of the frame.

Shaded Grounds

A shaded ground is a gradated wash of one hue. Start by preparing and organizing three to five graded tints or tones of a specific hue. Apply the lightest first, and introduce the successive grades of color as you work across and down the silk, ending with the darkest. After each change of color immediately go back and blend the color by rubbing your semidry brush back and forth where the shades overlap. Once the dye has started to dry, never apply more dye or attempt to change the color. This will cause water marks and streaking.

Ombrés

When blending an ombré of analogous colors (such as yellow to orange to brown), follow the same procedure used for one graded hue, except start with a clean brush and the lightest hue and work toward the darkest. You really need only one brush for this procedure. But if you are concerned that it may contaminate the different jars of dye, use a clean brush for each color and pay special attention to blending the color on the silk before changing brushes.

When painting large areas with light ground colors, use H. Dupont dye thinner or Tinfix diffusing agent as a dilutant rather than alcohol and water. These commercial dilutants help the dye flow and dry evenly. They can also be used to dilute the dye in order to make a tint or a shade. Like the alcohol dilutant, they can be applied directly to the silk before applying dye in order to keep the silk wet and workable.

Surface design © Susan L. Moyer.
This silhouette of a floral motif is painted over an ombré ground.

DEMONSTRATION:
Painting an Ombré

To facilitate speed, which is important when applying dye to broad, large areas on the silk, organize a tray with the dyes, foam brushes, and a container of dilutant. You may want to apply alcohol dilutant to the silk; this will make the colors blend more easily and give you more time to blend them before the silk dries.

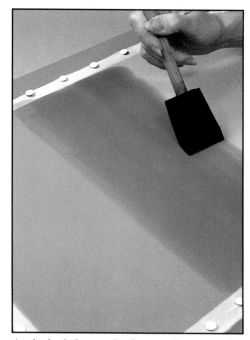

Apply the lightest color first, overlapping each brushstroke. Introduce the successive grades of color as you work across and down the silk, ending with the darkest.

After each change of color, immediately go back and blend the color by rubbing your semi-dry brush back and forth where the shades overlap.

This completed ombré shows the successful gradual blending of each color into the next.

BLOTCHES

Blotches are more difficult to paint evenly than most ground colors because of the careful brushwork needed to paint around intricate designs and in small areas. More than one edge has to be kept wet, and working this way requires a lot of time and concentration. If the working edges dry before the application of dye is completed, undesirable ridges of color and streaking will result.

There are steps you can take to avoid these technical difficulties. During the initial planning of the design, divide large areas into smaller sections by using design elements that intersect to subdivide larger areas. Also, to prevent the silk from drying too quickly, many silk painters wet the blotch area before applying the dye. Several wetting agents can be used for this: commercial dilutants that have been developed for this job, an alcohol and water solution, or distilled water. When you are applying light colors, the commercial dilutants render the most satisfactory results.

For painting large flat areas that are bordered by intricate motifs, use the large squirrel-hair quill brushes. They hold a lot of dye so that you can cover a large area with one broad stroke, and they come to a fine point that will easily go around and into the intricate areas.

When painting on dry silk, avoid accidentally flooding the dye over the gutta barrier by applying the dye a short distance from the gutta edge. Allow the dye to spread naturally toward the gutta line and into small and narrow areas through a process known as capillary attraction. When the dye is applied to wet silk it spreads more slowly than when applied to dry silk because the wetness of the fabric holds back the dye. This means that a slightly different technique is necessary. To avoid halos around the designs and motifs, be careful to paint the dye up to the gutta lines and into intricate areas.

To avoid smearing the dye, apply it from left to right if you are right-handed and vice versa if you are left-handed. For easy access, move the cup of dye close to the area that you are painting, or keep the cup in your free hand.

TIPS

• To make it easier to clean up leaks into a blotch area, paint the motif first and the blotch last. Leaks onto white silk can be repaired; leaks onto an already painted blotch are difficult to overcome or integrate into a design.

• When you are painting a blotch around an intricate motif, you may find it difficult to keep areas from drying before you finish applying the dye. Since this causes streaking and uneven color, try to recruit an assistant so you can keep all the edges working and cover twice as much area before the fabric dries. My husband, Dale, has become a very competent assistant.

• For ideas on how to develop a variety of textured grounds, refer to the sections on salt crystals, alcohol techniques, and line building (pages 102–119).

Lilies. © Susan L. Moyer. *This detail of a scarf was painted using the procedure demonstrated on the facing page. The sensuously drawn and delicately shaded lilies make a striking contrast to the flat horizontal stripes.*

DEMONSTRATION:
Painting a Blotch

Utilize the tip of a large squirrel-hair quill brush to paint around an intricate motif. Apply the dye a short distance from the gutta edge and allow the dye to flow from the brush toward the gutta line.

When painting the large flat areas of a blotch, use the large squirrel-hair quill brush, and paint with broad, even, overlapping brushstrokes.

This example shows the kinds of problems that can occur when you are painting a flat background around a motif, either on white silk or over a ground color. Note the unwanted ridges of dye connecting some of the motifs, and the streaks in the open areas. To prevent these technical problems, either steam-set the ground color before overpainting or recruit someone to help you keep all the working edges wet.

AVOIDING AND CORRECTING MISTAKES

Unwanted stains on a painting can be due to accidental drips, splashes, or technical mistakes. Breaks in the gutta barrier, an overloaded brush that floods the dye over a gutta line, or a brush tip that carelessly goes over the line can create unwanted color stains.

Dyes that have spread out of control can never be totally removed from the silk, especially those that react to the silk on contact, like Jacquard and a few Super Tinfix colors. But you can reduce the concentration of dye so that future applications of color will not spread and mix with the leaked dye to cause a bigger problem.

If the dye seeps through a break in the gutta barrier, you must act quickly to control the damage. Repair the line *immediately* with gutta both on the front and back of the silk. This will help prevent more dye from seeping through. (Sometimes the repair will not seal because the break is too large and the silk is too wet. If this is the case, let the area dry thoroughly, and then repair with gutta. But is has been my experience that a quick gutta repair will seal a *small* leak.) Quickly, using a cotton swab or clean brush, apply a barrier of alcohol around the renegade dye. The alcohol will push the dye back toward the gutta line and keep it from traveling any farther. Use a cotton swab to pick up as much color as you possibly can. Continue to dilute the dye with a brush as you pick up the color with a dry cotton swab. You will need to apply and pick up several applications of alcohol to effectively dilute the dye. (As you work, be careful not to drag a wet cotton swab over other areas of your design.)

When the silk is dry you may notice a dull patch on the fabric surface. Future applications of dye may not blend and dry evenly over these patches. To make the surface uniform, treat the whole surface to be dyed by applying an alcohol dilutant wash. After letting the dilutant wash dry, apply the dye, being careful to smooth out any unevenness by rubbing your brush back and forth. This will blend the edges of the patches and any residue of color left in the silk.

If the problem seems irreversible, such as a color bleeding onto a painted ground, you might consider changing the design to incorporate or cover up the flow. Minor flaws can be overpowered by the addition of a texture, such as salt, faux batik, or the alcohol textures. Lots of personal discoveries and beautiful results have grown out of inventive handling of such accidents.

TIPS

• Keep a gutta applicator, isopropyl alcohol, dilutant, and cotton swabs handy when you apply dye.

• Before applying dye, hold your painting up to the light and check the back of your silk to see if the resist has penetrated the silk. Make sure all starts and stops are connected and sealed.

• Before applying any dye, you may want to check for breaks in the resist by applying dilutant to the background or appropriate area of your design. If the dilutant leaks, wait for the silk to dry, and repair the resist before applying dye.

DEMONSTRATION: Correcting Mistakes

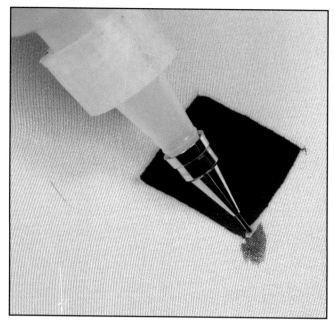

If dye seeps through a small break in the gutta line, halt its flow with a quick application of gutta.

Contain the dye by applying a ring of alcohol around the stain.

Next dilute the dye with a brushful of alcohol, and pick it up with a dry cotton swab. You will need to apply and pick up several applications of alcohol to dilute the dye effectively.

Compare this stain to the first picture. Notice how the concentration of dye has been significantly reduced but the alcohol has left a dull patch on the fabric. To make the surface uniform so that it will accept the next application of dye more evenly, treat the whole surface with an alcohol dilutant wash.

7: THE DIRECT METHOD

After mastering the gutta line and working within its limitations, you may feel as though gutta lines are controlling you, inhibiting your growth as a designer. There is another method of silk painting that allows you to paint directly on the silk without the use of a gutta line. The direct method, as this technique is sometimes referred to by the trade, will open up a whole new creative direction in silk painting.

The stretched silk is first treated with a solution of gutta and a solvent such as Turpenoid or mineral spirits. The gutta treatment creates a surface on the silk that prevents the dye from spreading. In essence, this silk painting technique is very similar to working with transparent watercolor on paper. If you are a watercolorist you may find you can adapt some of your techniques to the direct method of painting on silk. For example, try working wet-on-wet to create softly blended effects, applying wet and dry brushstrokes over dried grounds to build images and create form, lifting color to create special effects, or placing salt crystals on a painting just before it dries to create subtle textures. Accidental forms can be created by using a straw to blow a large spot of wet dye across the surface of the treated silk, and interesting textures can be created by applying dye with the soft irregular surface of a sponge.

Purple Floral Patch. © Sissi Siska.

PAINTING ON TREATED SILK

The silk you choose for direct painting should have a tight, flat weave. The tightness of the weave helps keep the gutta from forming puddles on the underside of the silk, and the smooth surface helps the brushstrokes of dye to maintain crisp edges instead of fuzzing.

When executing surface designs for the trade, Joanne Siska, whose work appears on page 88 and elsewhere in this book, prefers to work on 8-momme pongee. She has found that this particular weave and weight of silk absorbs the gutta treatment thoroughly and evenly, and the flat surface is easy to work on. For her decorative and fine art paintings, which include both wax and gutta treatment, she uses 14-momme crepe de chine. Although this silk is slightly more difficult to work on and expensive to treat because the heavier silk soaks up a lot of gutta and solvent, it also absorbs more dye than lightweight silks, giving a richness and depth to the color. Also, the durability of weave helps the silk withstand the harsh treatment it receives when Joanne applies several layers of resists, overdyeing, and intermediate steamings.

Ryl Nordquist, whose designs are also featured in this book, works on 12- and 14-momme pongee as well as 14- and 16-momme crepe de chine. Ryl does not wash or dry-clean the sizing out of the pongee before she applies the gutta treatment, because she has found that the sizing adds to the quality of the resist. Although Ryl has had success, her processes and silks may vary from yours, so be sure to test your dyes and processes on the silk before proceeding with a painting.

Crepe de chine is very elastic. Make sure it is stretched tightly to prevent sagging before you treat it with a gutta solution. The sagging will cause uneven absorption of the solution, which will make the dye form splotches.

Inspired by Redouté.
© *Nelida McCarty. This painting is an example of how a watercolorist adapted her techniques to create beautiful rendered and shaded roses on treated silk.*

84 • The Direct Method

MIXING THE GUTTA TREATMENT

Most professional silk painters use Turpenoid to mix their gutta treatment because, unlike mineral spirits, it is odorless and therefore easier to tolerate. Also, some artists feel that Turpenoid produces a more even and thorough application of gutta treatment on the silk because it is a more refined product than mineral spirits. The petroleum distillates contained in both these products should not be inhaled or absorbed through the skin and are combustible. Therefore, be sure to wear rubber gloves, and mix and apply the gutta treatment only in a well-ventilated space with an exhaust fan and away from any open flame.

Mix 2 parts Turpenoid to 1 part gutta (Sennelier, H. Dupont, or Jacquard) in a glass jar, with an opening big enough to receive 2-inch (5-cm) sponge brush. Cap the jar tightly and shake the mixture vigorously. Let the mixture sit a moment to allow the bubbles to rise and escape. The consistency of gutta can vary from one manufacturer to another, even from one container to another, so you may want to test your initial gutta treatment mixture made from a new can of gutta for effectiveness before starting a painting.

The gutta treatment may lose its full effectiveness if it is not used on the day it is mixed. If you find yourself with left-over gutta treatment, save it in a tightly capped glass jar. Before applying it to your silk, test its consistency again.

Over time, dried gutta treatment will discolor white silk. Treat only as much silk as you plan to paint within two weeks, and then steam and dry-clean your finished work.

To test the mixture, first using a gutta applicator and regular gutta to outline a small area about 4 inches square on a scrap of silk, and then apply the gutta treatment inside that area. Let the treatment dry on the silk in a well-ventilated room or outside. In order for the treatment to dry, the solvent must dissipate, leaving a thin layer of gutta on the silk. Depending on the atmospheric conditions, this may take an hour or several hours. Letting the silk dry outdoors is the safest method. If this is inconvenient, the alternative is to place your silk in front of an exhaust fan and dry the treatment using a hair dryer. This only takes a minute but you must be careful not to burn the silk or inhale the fumes. Do not attempt to dry a large piece of freshly treated silk with a hair dryer. It causes a billow of dangerous fumes, and the treatment may lose some of its effectiveness.

Once the treated silk is dry, you are ready to test it with dye. When you are choosing a color for this, it is helpful to know that different colors behave differently when they are applied to the silk. For example, Ryl has discovered that Tinfix turquoise and Super Tinfix black are a good pair for testing the effectiveness of your gutta mixture. If the edges of the black strokes are noticeably fuzzy or the dye is spreading on the silk, the gutta mixture is too thin. To remedy this problem, add more gutta to the gutta mixture. If the turquoise dye beads up on the treated silk and does not pentrate and dry evenly, the gutta mixture is too thick. Add more Turpenoid to the gutta mixture.

Some colors will bead up when first applied to the treated silk but will blend and dry evenly. This is just the behavior of certain colors, not necessarily a reflection on the quality of the gutta treatment.

DEMONSTRATION:
Adjusting the Consistency of Gutta Treatment

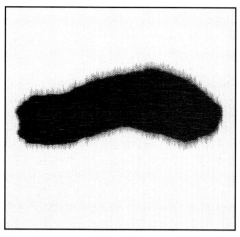

Tinfix black dye will fuzz if a gutta solution is too thin.

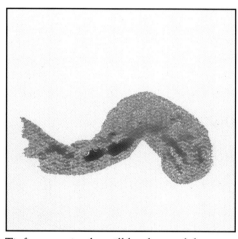

Tinfix turquoise dye will bead up and dry unevenly if the gutta treatment is too thick.

This example shows how the Tinfix black and turquoise should react if the treatment is the proper consistency for painting.

APPLYING THE GUTTA

Once you are satisfied with the consistency of your gutta mixture, use long, even strokes to apply the mixture to the stretched silk. The gutta should run off the foam brush quickly, and the brush should move easily on the silk. If the gutta mixture drags, it is too thick. You should hear a swishing sound as you apply the gutta. When you start a stroke, be careful not to apply too much pressure or have too much treatment on the brush. In either case, the gutta may push through the weave or puddle and run on the underside of your stretched silk. If this happens, wipe off the excess gutta treatment from your foam brush on the lip of the jar and carefully use the brush to pick up the drips from the underside of the silk. Work quickly because you should never go back over drying gutta with a brush or the gutta will thicken in areas and cause splotches in the painting. To keep the treatment even, allow the silk to dry in a flat position. When treating a large piece or several stretchers of silk at a time, it is best to work outdoors so that you will have plenty of ventilation. The gutta treatment is slightly photosensitive, so don't leave the treated silk to dry under dappled or moving shadows.

To apply gutta treatment to silk, work quickly and evenly with a large brush. Be sure to work in a well-ventilated area, and if possible, let the silk dry outside.

APPLYING COLOR

In the direct method, the dye does not flow off a brush and run freely as it would on untreated silk. The key to controlling the dye and creating texture is the brushes. Like watercolor paper, treated silk will take on the visual texture created by the painter's brushstrokes. Experiment with brushes of all shapes and sizes, and challenge yourself to create lively brushstrokes and exciting textures.

Before you undertake a major project, experiment with the behavior of the dyes. Each brand of dye and each color within a brand has a specific behavior. This behavior not only shows itself during the process of painting but continues through the steaming process. For example, concentrated blacks tend to fuzz during the steaming process if painted over fugitive colors (hot colors like Super Tinfix orchid and bergamote yellow). To help avoid this, be sure to dilute the superconcentrated dyes, but be aware that some colors may continue to fuzz even if they have been diluted. When painting Jacquard silk colors on treated silk, add a few drops of isopropyl alcohol to the dye so that it will penetrate the treatment. If you find that a pre-mixed color (such as H. Dupont Orchide #386) will not apply evenly on the gutta treatment, try changing the behavior of that color by mixing the color from stock dyes.

When you are working in humid conditions, the silk will retain moisture, causing a capillary attraction; therefore, the dyes will tend to bleed and fuzz more than under dry conditions. To avoid this problem, either wait till the weather changes if possible, or use a dehumidifier to remove the moisture in your studio, and dry your painting thoroughly between applications of color either with a diffuser or by placing your painting under a warm lamp.

As you paint on treated silk the dye is absorbed by the treatment and dries to a dull pastel, making it difficult to determine the value or intensity of your colors. Therefore, if you don't want to take the time to test your colors on untreated silk, it is helpful to mix your dyes in a white container (palette) so you can judge their color before using them. Once the colors are applied, you can determine their intensity while the dyes are still wet on the silk. After the painting has been steam-set and the gutta treatment has been dry-cleaned out of the silk, the colors will be more intense and appear as they did when wet.

If your painting calls for washes of one or several blended colors, apply them first. Applying isopropyl alcohol to treated silk will create soft washes for an effect similar to that achieved by first wetting watercolor paper before applying color. The alcohol penetrates the gutta and wets the silk, allowing the dye to blend and dry with soft edges. Use a foam brush to apply the alcohol in the areas where you plan to apply your color wash. Be careful not to create puddles of alcohol. Let the alcohol dry a moment until the wet and shiny silk turns to a dull finish. Then apply a wash of color. As with watercolor, building up washes of dye on treated silk requires skill. The wetness of the fabric will determine the crispness or softness of the painted edge. After the wash of color has dried, the treated silk will again hold a sharp edge so that you can paint over the dry background color with details and accents. For example, in the initial stages of a floral design, the surface designer will use wet-on-wet washes of color to create

DEMONSTRATION: Painting Details onto a Treated Ground

As a last step in painting the lily, gutta treatment is applied over the whole flower and left to dry. Before applying gutta treatment, make sure your design is finished except for the final details.

Details can now be painted directly onto the silk, such as the spots on the petals of the lily. This technique is very similar to using a dry brush to apply the finishing touches to a watercolor.

© Joanne Siska. This detail of a surface design is a clear example of how an artist builds a design on treated silk. First Joanne applied washes to a wet ground and then added details with a dry brush on a dry surface.

an airy, light background and to capture the delicacy of petals and leaves. Once the silk has dried, a dry brush gives the flowers and leaves form and definition.

Colors tend to bleed and blend somewhat when applied next to each other, making crisp delineations between colors difficult. Nonetheless, using treated silk to paint detailed designs or renderings that have a lot of blending, shading, and drawing can be very rewarding. (See the piece by one of my students on page 84.)

To minimize bleeding, let one color dry before placing another next to it. But be aware that in some cases it is not the nature of this technique to maintain hard-edged delineations between colors. The French dyes contain alcohol, which momentarily weakens the gutta; besides, dyes are not permanent until they are steam-set. Therefore, when you are working with a large brush that is full of dye, the sheer quantity of dye and alcohol being applied will lift dye and make the colors

blend together, even if you let your colors dry thoroughly between applications. Through experimentation, you will be able to make the bleeding and blending become an integral part of your work.

When blending colors you may find it helpful to know that the behavior of the colors changes when alcohol dilutants are added to dyes. The more alcohol in a color, the more that color will repel the one next to it. Thus pastels will repel each other, but dark colors will blend more easily. To blend and mix colors on the silk, quickly rinse and blot your brush and continue to paint while the silk is still wet from the previous brushstroke of dye. When the blending of a color has reached the desired effect, you can preserve it by applying low heat from a hair dryer. You can also use a blow dryer or diffuser to help maintain crisp edges, or a dry-brush effect; dry the painting before applying more color. The hair dryer is a creative tool that can help you manipulate effects.

DEMONSTRATION: Creating a Soft Wash of Color

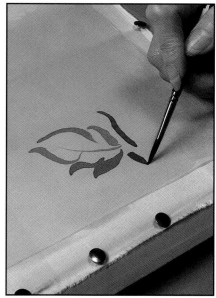

To create a soft wash on gutta-treated silk, first brush on alcohol or alcohol dilutant with a large brush. The surface should be evenly damp but without puddles.

Now apply dye wet-on-wet. The result will be a tinted wash with soft edges, quite similar to the kind achievable with watercolor on wet paper. As the alcohol dries, the color you apply will bleed less and less.

Once such a wash has dried, you can create contrasting crisp brushstrokes over the soft ground. Use any watercolor brush, and don't overload your brush with dye. The drier the silk, the crisper the edge.

TIPS

• When painted on treated silk, the dye does not penetrate evenly to the back of the silk. The underside will be dull and uneven in color, thus making direct painting an impractical technique for scarves and banners where both sides of the silk are visible.

• The dye tends to take unevenly on large flat areas. With this in mind, either apply the ground color first and then apply the treatment over it, or eliminate large flat areas when planning a painting.

• For even more design flexibility, hot wax can be applied on treated silk. See pages 128–129 for more information about this technique.

• Alcohol dilutant and cotton swabs can be used to remove color from the silk. To utilize this technique creatively, refer to page 115.

• For variety and flexibility in design, try applying the gutta treatment over a lightly colored or textured ground. Let the treatment dry, and then continue painting your design. *Note:* If you are planning to use intense colors such as Super Tinfix orient red, orchid, or intense bergamote yellow for ground colors, to avoid fuzzing when overpainting you must steam-set your dyes before applying the gutta treatment.

• The newly formulated Jacquard silk colors show promise for working exceptionally well when painted on treated silk. Since they react with the silk on contact, they tend to bleed less than the other dyes. Just remember to add at least a few drops of isopropyl alcohol to the dyes, which acts as a gutta solvent and helps the dyes penetrate the treated silk.

• *Caution:* Do not apply the treatment over colored guttas. The solvent in the solution will cause the colored guttas to dissolve and smear.

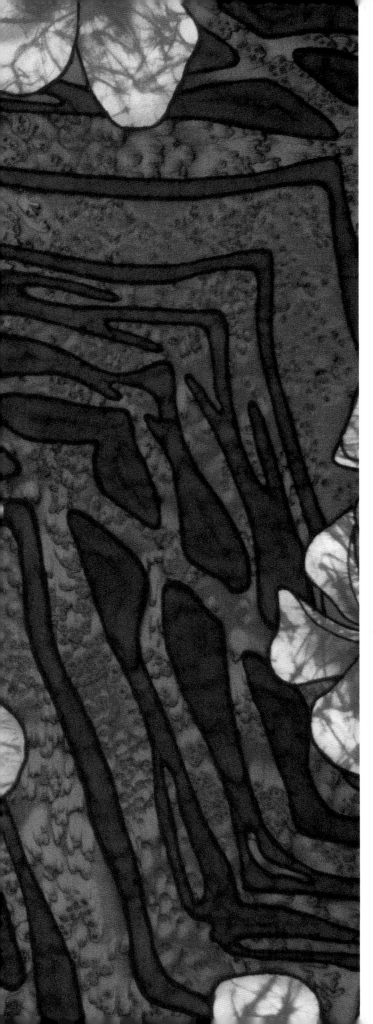

8: WAX RESIST TECHNIQUES

Wax is very versatile resist and impermeable to dye. When melted it becomes very fluid and easy to apply in a painterly or linear way with a variety of tools. Each tool or brush adds its own character to the quality of the line or brushstroke. Wax can also be applied to create a visual texture by using sponges, splatters, or drips, or by cracking the wax on the silk to produce a lacy network of fine lines.

For silk painters and surface designers the wax resist process has been effectively adapted to contemporary methods and materials. Wax can now be used as a resist with silk dyes applied directly, eliminating the successive dye baths required for traditional batik. This new approach affords unlimited coloration and total control over the cracking. If the cracking is desired in order to create the effect of a traditional batik or for added dimension and texture interest in a design or painting, it can be achieved by a process called faux batik.

Hawaiian Diagonal. © *Susan L. Moyer.*

THE WAX RESIST PROCESS

The use of wax as a resist adds an extra dimension to a design, especially when you are overdyeing the silk—that is, applying one color over another. Overdyeing is a technique for adding or altering color, and wax can be used in a painterly way to resist the new dye only in those places where you want to keep the old, lighter color. For example, if blue is applied over yellow, the yellow that is protected by the wax will remain yellow (say, bright flowers) while the rest of the yellow mixes with the blue dye and turns green (say, leaves surrounding them).

Both wax and gutta can be used as a resist for overdyeing. However, the painterly quality of hot wax makes it more versatile and effective. Consider the difference between using a fine gutta line to outline a leaf and using one stylized brushstroke of wax to indicate the leaf itself.

Gutta, in comparison to wax, is used either as a linear barrier resist or to treat the entire surface for painting in the direct method. Gutta's sticky consistency makes it difficult to

apply except through an applicator, but for intricate work the delicate gutta line is easier to control and apply than a wax line.

The original wax resist technique is called batik. The traditional batiks from Java were dyed with rich vegetable colors by submerging the waxed cloth into successive dye baths. The agitation of the cloth during the dyeing process caused the wax resist to crack, allowing the dye to be absorbed along the cracks into the cloth fibers. If there were more than a few cracks in the design, the batik was considered poorly crafted because the crack lines would obscure the intricate design. However, the delicate veining of cracked wax is now the most characteristic and prized feature in contemporary batiks found in home furnishings and apparel. The cracks give batik its distinctive look.

Faux batik is a controlled textural effect achieved by applying wax, cracking the wax, and applying dye, which is subsequently absorbed by the silk wherever it is exposed through the cracks.

Wax is very resistant to water and dye, and it effectively penetrates most silks, including textured weaves. Beeswax and paraffin have different qualities and are often combined to customize a resist. Beeswax is the most resilient and pliable resist and does not crack easily. This pliability makes cracking the wax for a textured effect more controllable. Paraffin is brittle and cracks easily. If handled roughly, paraffin tends to flake and peel, exposing the surface of the silk to too much dye. I suggest experimenting with a mixture of these waxes until you find the proportion that suits your needs. For faux batik, I use 1 part beeswax to 1 part paraffin. This combination gives me a good resist and a refined crackle. When I am designing and painting with a wax resist and I do not plan to incorporate the faux batik crackle in the design, I use 5 parts paraffin to 1 part beeswax. This resist is easily cleaned of any dye residue, and it is cheaper than pure beeswax.

Since wax is flammable and has the potential for emitting dangerous fumes, setting up to work with wax takes careful planning. Beeswax has a flash point of 450°F (232°C) and paraffin wax has a flash point of 400°F (204°C). For safety as well as ease of application, the wax should be melted and maintained at a temperature of no higher than 250°F (121°C). If the wax becomes overheated, potentially hazardous vapors will be emitted and the excessive heat will damage and discolor your silk. I recommend melting wax in an electric frying pan that has a built-in temperature control.

Also, when working with molten wax, ventilation is a primary consideration. Distributors of wax do not recommend the use of hot paraffin wax even in a well-ventilated area when infants or young children are present. The fumes from petroleum-based wax (paraffin) can be potentially hazardous to their immature respiratory and immune systems. If this is a consideration for you, work with natural beeswax.

Beeswax can be purchased from suppliers, either bleached or natural, in one-pound blocks. Any color or odor from the natural beeswax is removed from the silk during the dry-cleaning process. Paraffin wax is sold by the pound and can be purchased in the supermarket or from suppliers.

Birds of Paradise Batik.
© Susan L. Moyer.
The faux batik connects what would have been a rather disjointed design, adding depth, interest, and texture.

BRUSH APPLICATION

Wax is impossible to remove from a brush. With this in mind, set aside brushes for this job. When applying hot wax for faux batik, you will need only two brushes: a wooden-handled sponge brush for the large areas and a bamboo brush that holds a point for detail and intricate areas.

If you are using hot wax in a painterly way and as a resist for layering (you can layer the wax, or the colors, or both), a variety of brushes can be used. Each brush will lend its own character to the painting. Sissi Siska has what she calls her "funny brush," which looks as if it has been electrocuted. The hairs go in every direction, creating a dry-brush effect when used to apply wax. Ideally, brushes for applying wax should have wooden handles. Plastic may melt in the hot wax, and a brush with a metal ferrule will conduct heat and burn your hand. If you must use such a brush, insulate your hand from the heat by covering the clean ferrule with a few layers of masking tape before you dip the brush into the hot wax.

To keep your brushes from slipping into the wax pot, wind masking tape around the handle as many revolutions as needed to build up a ridge that will catch on the sides of the electric frying pan. Never leave your brushes in the wax pot for long periods of time. They will burn and become frizzy and misshapen. Also, remember to remove your brushes from the wax pot before turning the heat off. If you need to remove the wax from the frying pan, the easiest way is to let the wax cool until it is hard, then momentarily turn on the pan until the sides of the wax melt just enough to slide the wax out of the pan in one piece.

ELECTRIC WAX APPLICATORS

Wax applicators are special tools for drawing fluid wax lines that look similar to gutta lines. The heating units make it possible to maintain the wax at a constant temperature so that it flows evenly. The small electric wax pen, traditionally used for decorating eggs in the Ukraine, is a great tool for drawing detail and fine lines on silk. Tips in a range of different sizes can be purchased for the pen. Although the pen is easy to use, it must be refilled with wax frequently. This pen is most effective when used for controlled detailed work.

The electric tjanting has a large brass bowl that holds a lot more wax than the small electric pen. These bowls come with spouts of different sizes; some have two spouts. The electric tjanting lends itself to a fluid, linear batik effect and will apply a good resist to heavy-weight fabrics or a decorative resist line to treated silk. It takes a bit of practice with the tjanting before it can be used effectively.

Hot wax flows quickly out of the tjanting or off the brush, whereas gutta must be squeezed out of the applicator. Therefore wax must be applied with a steady, rhythmic movement. Keep a paper towel in your free hand to catch drips of wax that form while you are hesitating or repositioning the tjanting or wax pen. To ensure a good resist, the wax must penetrate the silk. When properly applied the dried wax should appear translucent when held to the light. If the wax appears flaky or white, chances are it is not hot enough and has not penetrated the silk properly. The tricks are to keep the molten wax at a constant temperature, to apply it in a smooth rhythmic motion, and to work on dry silk.

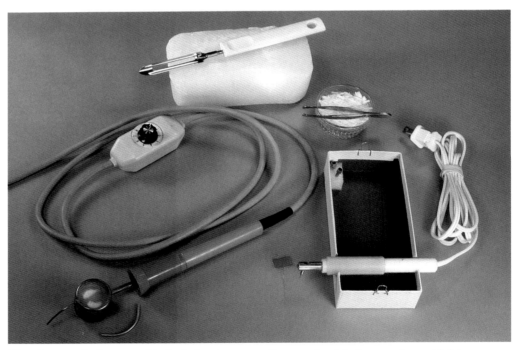

This photograph shows two kinds of electric wax applicators. At right is a wax pen; at left is a tjanting. Both can be fitted with different sizes of spouts. In the background are a block of beeswax, a paring tool for scraping off pieces of wax, and a bowl of wax shavings ready to be rolled into a small ball and placed into the wax pen with a pair of tweezers. To keep the cord of an electric applicator out of the way, either plug it into the ceiling outlet or suspend it overhead with a string.

FAUX BATIK

Adding a batik texture is the last step in the designing and painting process. The batik texture can cover the entire piece, the background, or just a section for detail. If you want to integrate the batik texture into the entire design, use a large sponge brush and cover the silk painting with the hot wax. Work quickly, returning the brush frequently to the wax pot to keep the wax hot and flowing. Check the back of your work to see whether the wax has penetrated and sealed the silk fibers so that they will resist the dye. If the wax is not penetrating, the molten wax in the pan may not be hot enough, or you may have let the wax on the brush cool too long before it reached the fabric. If the wax has not penetrated to the back side of the silk, complete the seal by brushing molten wax on the back of the stretched silk. When the wax has cooled, which takes only a few seconds, remove the silk from the frame and crack the wax by carefully and lightly crushing the piece as if you where crushing a piece of paper intended for the circular file. Too much crushing will create a muddy effect, so proceed carefully. When you have finished cracking the wax, unfold the silk and place it on a layer of clean newsprint or newspaper. Brush the dye directly onto the piece. It will be absorbed into the cracks and bead up on the wax. If you do not want the beaded texture on your finished painting, mop up the excess dye with an absorbent paper towel. To remove any smudging, wet the paper towel with a little alcohol.

To limit the batik texture only to certain areas of the design, apply wax only on the areas where you want the texture.

Remove the work from the frame and carefully crack the wax. Unfold the silk and tack the work back onto the frame. Now wax over the areas of the design where you don't want the cracked texture. The wax will seal and protect those areas from the dye. Then proceed by painting the dye over the work, mopping up the excess as you go. If there is any unwanted haze of color left on small areas of the wax surface, it can be wiped off with an alcohol-dampened cotton ball or swab. Let the silk dry.

Removing the Wax from the Silk

There are two methods of removing most of the wax from the silk. The traditional way is to place the batik between layers of newspaper that is at least 30 days old. (The aging precents the inks from transferring onto the design.) With an old dry iron, melt the wax into the newspaper, changing the layers of newspaper until they don't blot up much wax. This step is actually unnecessary, however, because wax can also be removed from the silk during the steaming process used to set the dyes. This is a very efficient way of removing wax because it eliminates the time and energy needed to do the ironing, as well as the mess and the fumes. If you are steaming other paintings along with a wax-laden one, protect the others from absorbing the melted wax by placing the waxed painting between several layers of newsprint. (Refer to pages 134–137 for detailed instructions and cautions.) Once the wax has been ironed or steamed out of the silk, the silk will be stiff and discolored with a wax residue. This stiff residue will be removed by the dry-cleaning process.

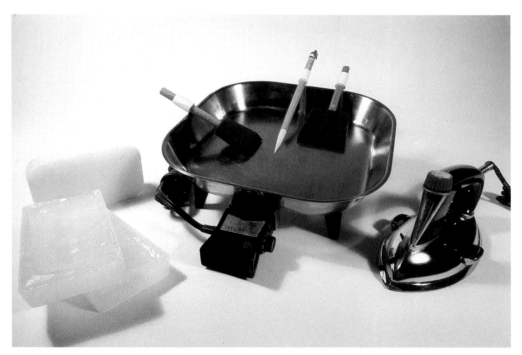

This photograph shows chunks of paraffin and beeswax, an electric frying pan for melting and controlling the temperature of wax, two wooden-handled foam brushes, a bamboo brush with a point for applying hot wax, and an iron for removing wax from the silk through several layers of clean newsprint. The ridges of masking tape on the brush handles prevent the brushes from sliding into the wax pot.

DEMONSTRATION: Faux Batik

Faux batik adds a texture that can be used to create the illusion of depth in a design.

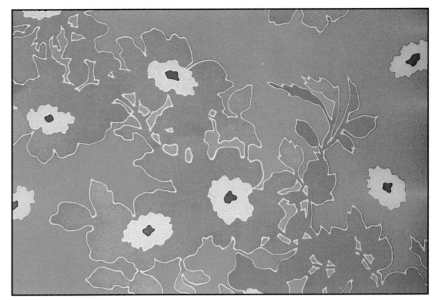

Here is a design executed with gutta on silk.

Hot wax was applied over the blue areas of the design. Once the wax had cooled, the silk was removed from its frame and gently crumpled so that the wax cracked in a random pattern. (Don't overdo the crumpling; too many cracks produce a muddy texture.)

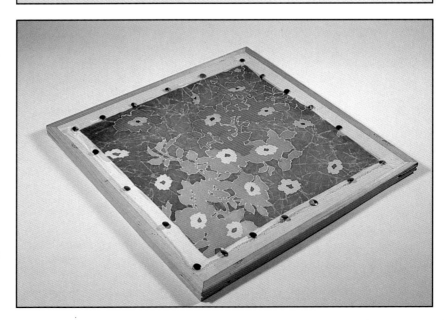

Next the silk was put back into its frame, and a protective layer of wax was painted over the pink and yellow motif but not the background. Here you can see this step partially completed; the pink flowers look darker where they already have been coated with wax.

Now a dark blue is painted over the entire design. The flowers will be completely protected by uncracked wax, but the dye will seep through the cracks in the background.

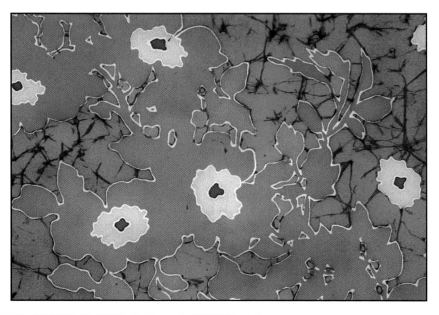

Most of the excess dye is removed with an absorbent paper towel. Any remaining residue can be removed with an alcohol-dampened paper towel or cotton swab. (Be sure to wear rubber gloves to protect your hands from the dye!)

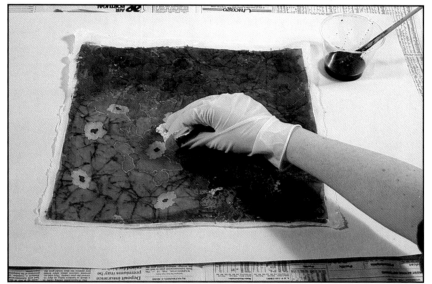

The simplest way to remove wax is to let it melt and be absorbed into several layers of newsprint during the steam-fixing process. (But you may want to partially remove heavy layers of wax before steaming by ironing the silk between several layers of clean newsprint.) In either case the remaining wax residue will be removed during dry cleaning.

The finished design shows an undisturbed floral motif against a textured background—an effect that would be very difficult to achieve in any other way.

Van Gogh Trees. *© Sissi Siska. Photo by Carol Seitz. Inspired by van Gogh, Sissi used successive brushstrokes of wax and dye to build the expressive elements in her design. The jacquard silk added even more texture.*

Enlarged Feather. © Sissi Siska. This dramatic painting effectively uses permanent black gutta to delineate the feathers and wax resist for texture.

Navajo Patchwork. © Sissi Siska. The colorful patches were outlined in permanent black gutta and then painted. The rest of the design was executed in wax and then overpainted with black dye.

Patchwork. © *Sissi Siska. This design cleverly incorporates wax resist and a variation of faux batik. The white areas were waxed out and then red dye was dropped into the triangle. The red triangle was preserved with wax, and the waxed areas were then cracked to produce a batik texture. The background was painted in several colors. Next the background patterns were drawn in wax on the colored ground, and the entire design was then overpainted in a dark color.*

Surface design © Ryl Nordquest. Ryl painted her leaves and flowers on treated silk. Before applying a sponge texture to the entire design, she preserved the floral motif with wax resist.

Harlequin Brushstrokes.
© 1991 Joanne Siska. This striking design is an example of how the wax brushstroke can be used as a design element. When black dye is overpainted, it may fuzz during the steaming process. For this reason the diamonds were steam-fixed before the last application of wax and black dye. Since dye will penetrate the silk again once the wax has been steamed out, the intermittent steaming let Joanne add another dimension to her design.

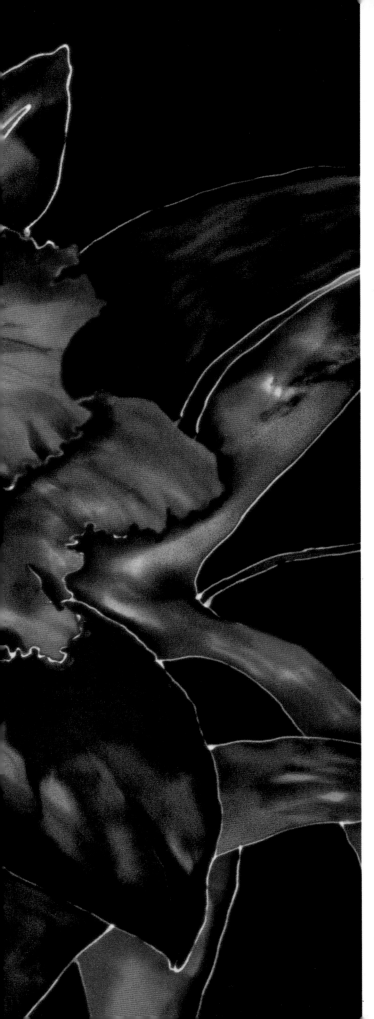

9: SPECIAL SUPPLEMENTARY TECHNIQUES

Silk painters use several techniques to create special effects. Salt crystals provide an intriguing pattern of colored swirls. Many interesting textures are possible with carefully controlled use of alcohol to push dye around on the dry silk. Painting wet-on-wet by applying color on a wet ground will create soft shapes and patterns. And the line building technique can be used to imitate the look of rows of misty mountains receding into the distance.

These techniques and the others discussed in this section are excellent ways to create a textured ground that the artist then paints over, or a planned texture within a specific area of a painting. These special supplementary techniques can be used to create beautiful paintings without the use of a resist. All of these techniques should be within the versatile silk painter's repertoire.

Midnight Orchid. © *Suzanne Punch.*

THE SALT CRYSTAL TECHNIQUE

The main principle behind this technique is that salt attracts and absorbs moisture. When salt crystals are placed on freshly painted silk, the salt will pull the wet dye in various directions, creating undulating swirls and shapes. Control of this texture develops as you become familiar with your dyes and how they react. Each brand of dye, as well as colors within a brand, can react differently to the salt crystals. Of the two brands of French dye, H. Dupont and Sennelier, H. Dupont gives the most dramatic results.

Salt crystals work best on strong to medium values of color, either one color or a combination of colors. Pastel colors are too weak to create a dramatic texture. Try using sea salt, kosher salt, table salt, or rock salt. The various sizes of crystals pull the dye in varying degrees, creating different effects.

The variety of movement and density in a texture is affected by several factors: the number and size of the salt crystals; their placement on the silk; the type of dye and intensity of the color; the weight, weave, and wetness of the silk; the tilt of the frame during the drying process; and the temperature, humidity, and drafts in your studio. Always remember to test colors and values you are unfamiliar with to see how they yield to the pull of the salt crystals.

You can incorporate the salt technique into a design with other silk-painting techniques. In the artwork on the following pages, for example, the salt technique has been incorporated as a textured blotch or ground, and to bring textural interest into a motif or abstract design.

When you are steaming work that incorporates the salt technique, the salt residue will continue to attract moisture. If not handled properly, the work will bleed and possibly be damaged or damage other work in the steamer. To avoid problems, protect the work by layering it between two sheets of plain newsprint. Then roll it with the other work as demonstrated on pages 134–137.

You can use the salt technique to create a textured ground and then use gutta and other silk-painting techniques on top of it. Here are a few technical considerations for doing this.

Before applying gutta to a salt-textured ground, let the color dry thoroughly. Then carefully remove and dispose of all the salt crystals. The salt residue may make the silk rough in places, interfering with the application of gutta lines. Also, the residue may continue to pull the second application of dye over the gutta lines. To avoid this, apply heavy gutta lines. If necessary, adjust the consistency of the gutta so that it penetrates the silk properly.

Because the dyes are transparent, when you apply a color over a salt-textured ground it takes on the texture of that ground. This produces a very interesting effect that should be considered part of the technique. Also, there is usually enough salt residue left on the ground to create a small pulling effect when you apply a second color, so don't expect color to go down evenly on the silk.

Your brush will pick up some salt residue and contaminate the dyes you are using. Dye contaminated with salt residue will not go down evenly. Label and set aside any leftover dye for future projects that incorporate the salt technique, or discard any unused contaminated dye. Never pour the unused portion back into your stock colors.

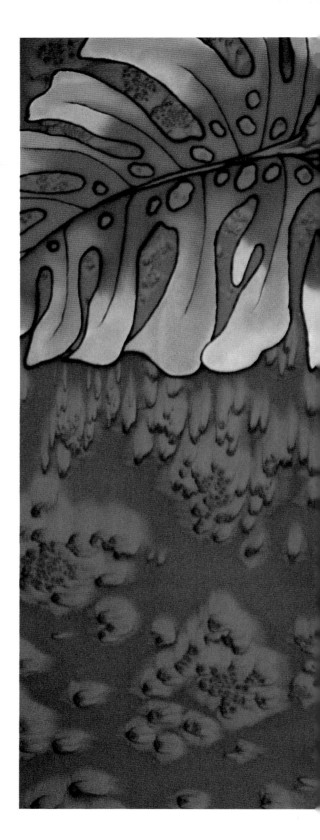

Tropical Leaf. © *Susan L. Moyer. Although the salt texture is difficult to translate and reproduce in a textile print, this salt-textured background was used to add interest to this swimwear design.*

Grisaille Peonies. *© Suzanne Punch. This painting incorporates the alcohol and shading techniques, which develop the form in the flowers, and the salt technique, which adds an interesting texture to the background.*

DEMONSTRATION: Salt Crystals

The salt technique is a realistic approach to yardage for fashions and home furnishings since the artist can create a salt texture on large areas of fabric in a relatively short time.

To create a salt texture, coarse sea salt was placed on a very wet ombré ground. Notice that the crystals are not thrown onto the silk but rather carefully placed in a random pattern.

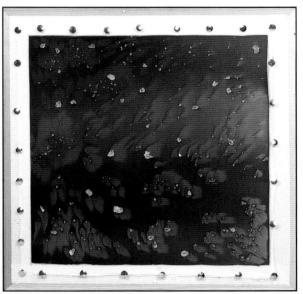

Here the salt crystals have started to pull the wet dye to create a very effective texture.

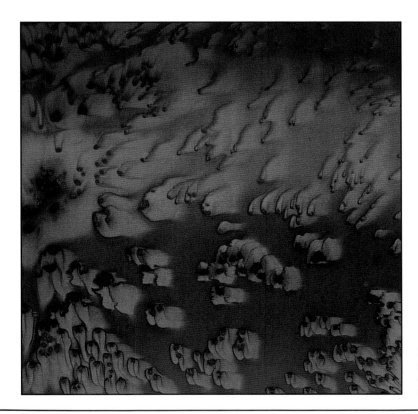

Once the dye is dry and the texture is fully developed, the salt crystals were carefully removed and discarded leaving a ground texture as you see here.

Textured Flowers. © Susan L. Moyer. In this floral design the salt texture motifs were painted over a pure pastel ground. Notice the range of color that can be achieved even when overpainting on a bright pink ground.

Angel Fish. *© Susan L. Moyer. This painting is an example of how various dyes react to salt differently. H. Dupont dyes were used for the violet and emerald, and Super Tinfix lagoon blue was used for the center diagonal. Since lagoon blue did not react with the salt and I wanted a texture in this area, I used a sponge to apply a texture with gutta and then carefully overpainted with a second coat of lagoon blue.*

THE ALCOHOL TECHNIQUE

Droplets of liquid splattering from your brush can stain and ruin a silk painting. Unplanned and uncontrolled, it is a studio nightmare. On the other hand, droplets of alcohol dilutant that are controlled can create a variety of effective and useful techniques.

As a droplet of alcohol (pure or diluted with water) spreads into a spot on a painted ground, it pushes the dye to the outer edge of the spot, creating a thin ring of darker color around the spot. The spot, when dry, is lighter than the ground color, and the outer ring is slightly darker. In essence, you are using dilutant to push the dye around. If this is done in a systematic way, with a design direction in mind, a variety of magnificent textures and painterly effects can be developed.

It is best to start with a dry ground that has a medium to strong application of dye. (Pastel tints do not contain enough dye to produce a texture.) The ground can be a flat color, shaded, variegated, or an ombré of analogous colors. It is always wise to test a color to judge whether or not the dye can be manipulated. To do so, dip a clean, pointed brush into a small container of the alcohol dilutant. Let the point of the brush momentarily touch a sample piece of dry, painted silk. Observe whether the dye is being pushed to the outer edge of the spot, creating a concentrated ring of dye. Some colors, such as the Super Tinfix primaries (blue lagoon, orchid, and bergamote yellow) and Jacquard silk colors such as carmine red, are not easily pushed around. H. Dupont dyes work the best, so experiment with several colors before you decide on a palette.

The size of the brush, the amount of alcohol or dilutant on the brush, and the length of time you hold the brush to the silk will determine the size of the spot or shape. This technique can easily be controlled with a little practice. Once you have some control, try creating a texture by following a system like the one demonstrated below.

I often use droplets to create interest in a design. They don't have to disappear into an overall texture to be useful. Droplets can represent clichés such as bubbles in an underwater design theme or morning dew on the petals of a flower, or they can be simply another abstract design element.

For variety of technique, the dye surface can be manipulated with brushstrokes of the alcohol dilutant to create form and texture. Suzanne Punch, a master of this alcohol technique, gives life and form to her exquisite flowers by manipulating the dyes with brushstrokes of the alcohol dilutant. Suzanne works back into the flower with several applications of alcohol dilutant and dye until she achieves the desired effect. She has found that the effect of moving the color is more pronounced if the dye is thoroughly dry before she applies the alcohol. For an added painterly effect, she also applies brushstrokes of color over dry color.

By experimenting with brushstrokes of the alcohol dilutant and color on dry silk, you will discover exciting effects that you may want to incorporate into your design work.

DEMONSTRATION: Creating a Texture with Droplets

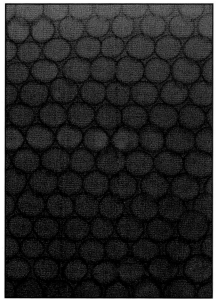 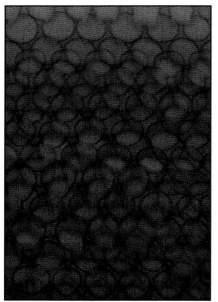 

On a painted ground, use the alcohol and water solution to make a row of spots that touch one another. Next to the first row of spots, make another row, staggering the spots from row to row until the desired area is covered, as in the left box above.

Now place spots into the areas where three spots touch, creating a row of spots that overlaps the first layer of spots. Follow the system of staggering the spots until you have covered the area, as in the right box above.

Overlap the first two layers of spots with more rows of spots, staggering them as you go. Repeat this system until the individual spots have disappeared into an overall texture.

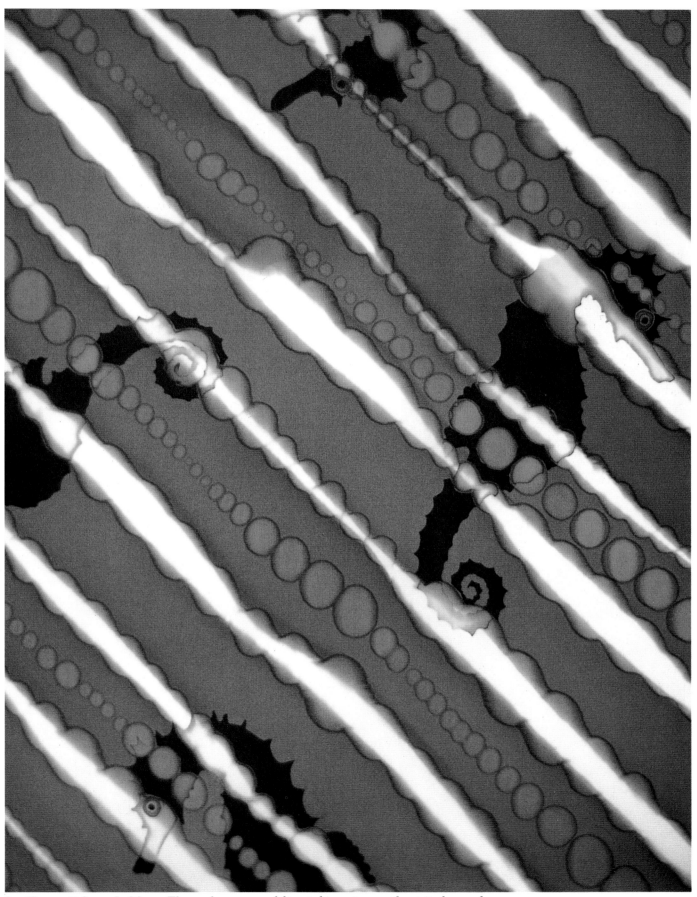

Sea Horses. © Susan L. Moyer. *The sea horses were delineated in gutta over the striped ground.*
Then alcohol techniques and dye were used to build the image and give the sea horses an underwater effect.

THE WET-ON-WET TECHNIQUE

The wet-on-wet technique is a special effect often used as a foundation or ground for layering. On silk wet with alcohol dilutant, colors can be blended to create a soft pastel ground, or the dyes can be applied in a pattern of shapes as illustrated here. Apply the alcohol dilutant to the silk, and then apply the dye over the dilutant. The alcohol solution retards the flow of dye so that patterns and shapes of color can be applied to the silk. The shapes of color spread slowly, drying with a soft edge.

This technique works very well for designs that superimpose contrasting design elements, such as soft and hard edges. For example, try creating a soft-edged background with the alcohol technique and then using wax resist over it. The contrasting textures can be integrated quite effectively into one overall design.

Surface design © Gay Lynette Morris. To execute this interesting design, Gay used the technique demonstrated on the facing page. She applied her colors to a wet ground and let them bleed to a soft edge. Once the silk was dry she used a resist to draw the grid of square flowers and then carefully overpainted the design with black dye.

DEMONSTRATION:
Wet-on-Wet

First alcohol dilutant is applied to the silk. While the silk is wet, dye is applied. The dye will spread and dry with a soft edge. The more alcohol, the less the dye will spread.

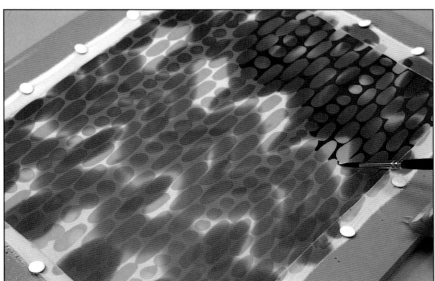

After the silk is dry, rounded shapes of hot wax are applied with a sable round brush designated for this purpose only. Then dark dye is painted around the wax shapes.

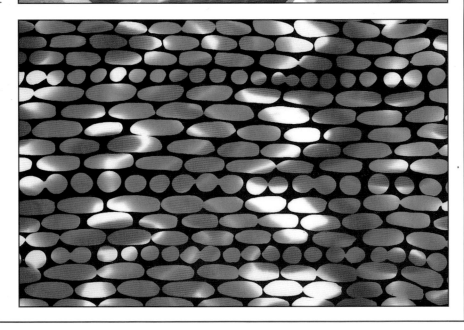

Here is the finished design.

DEMONSTRATION: Retaining White Areas

Here alcohol dilutant is being applied to the silk in the areas where white is desired.

When dye is applied next to the alcohol dilutant it does not flow into the white, but creates a soft edge.

Now coarse salt is sprinkled over the silk while the alcohol and dyes are still wet.

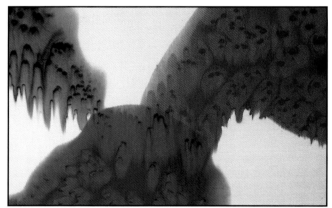

This detail of the finished painting shows the soft, sometimes wavy edges created when the salt pulls the dye into the white areas covered with alcohol dilutant. As you experiment you will find that this technique will produce some very interesting and dramatic effects.

RETAINING WHITE AREAS WITH ALCOHOL

Alcohol dilutant applied to a dry area of silk tends to repel dye applied next to it and keep the dye from flowing into the area. The edges, where the color mixes with the alcohol, are softened so that the color looks integrated into the white areas instead of applied and hard-edged. In essence, use the alcohol dilutant as if it were white dye. For example, to keep white in a design when applying a salt-textured ground, apply the dilutant in the area you want to keep white just before you apply the dye. The wet area will repel the next application of dye from flowing onto the white silk.

The secret of success with this technique, especially when adding the salt texture, is to be sloppy and freely blend the dye and alcohol dilutant.

ALCOHOL ON TREATED SILK

When you are working on gutta-treated silk in the direct method of silk painting, alcohol dilutant can be used to pick up and remove color. (See examples on facing page.)

Soon after the dye is dry (no more than an hour after applying it), add the alcohol dilutant from a squirt bottle in drops and lines, or from a brush. Pick up the excess alcohol dilutant with a cotton swab. Color will be removed with the solution to leave a light shape. For best results, remove the dye before it has time to stain the silk permanently. (The longer the dye dries on the fabric, the harder it is to remove, even without steam setting. Different colors behave differently, so experiment first.) When incorporating this technique, allow yourself enough time to complete a project in one sitting.

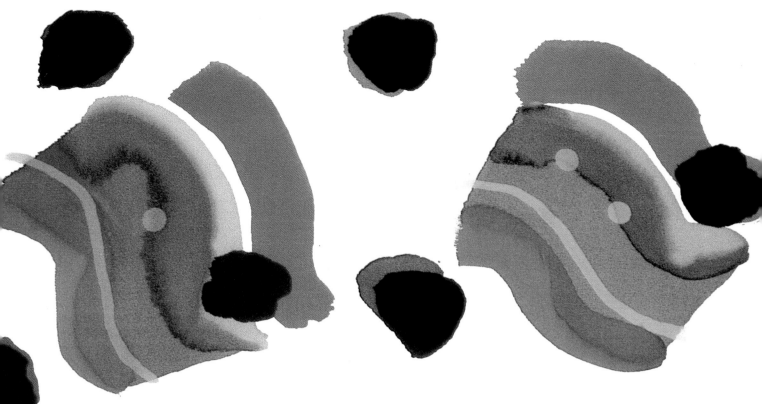

Surface design © Susan L. Moyer. Here I used the alcohol technique, which removes color from gutta-treated silk, to draw lighter dots and lines on the brushstrokes of dye.

DEMONSTRATION:
Alcohol on Gutta-Treated Silk

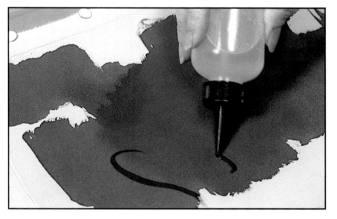

First apply dye to treated silk. Once it is dry, use a plastic squeeze bottle filled with alcohol dilutant to squirt lines and dots onto the treated silk.

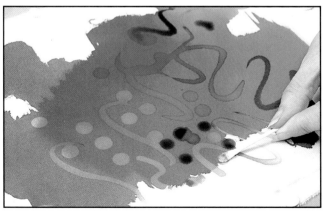

After only a few moments, use cotton swabs to absorb and remove the dilutant and dye, leaving behind a light shape. Wherever the dilutant is applied, the dye lifts and travels in the wet solution. When the dilutant is then absorbed and picked up by a cotton swab, colored swirls are left on the white. Have fun experimenting!

LINE BUILDING TECHNIQUES

Mountains in the mist, sand dunes, cliffs, wave prints on the sand, abstract textures—these are some of the special visual effects you can achieve by applying a controlled amount of dye to dry silk. Allow the dye to spread and dry naturally (that is, without the use of treated silk or a linear resist to restrain it), and dark ridges of color will form along the edges of the color. These dark ridges of color can be used to create a special effect called line building.

The first step in line building is to apply a light ground color to the silk. Allow the ground to dry thoroughly. Then apply a darker shade of dye (either the same hue or a different one) and allow at least one edge to travel naturally on the silk. When the dye stops flowing, a ridge of concentrated dye will appear. You can either let the dye stop naturally or interrupt its flow by applying low heat from a hair dryer.

Each subsequent color applied should be darker in value and cover a subsequently smaller area of the ground. Always allow the dye to dry thoroughly between applications.

Experiment by using line building as a ground under gutta treatment. If you plan to do this, it is wise to keep your colors light or bright.

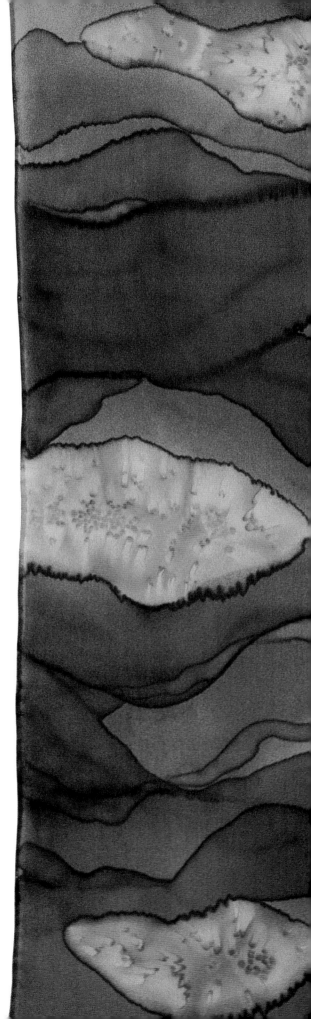

Scarves © Joan Berglund. The detail of the scarf on the right was created by line building over a light blue ground color. Once Joan finished her line building, she added areas of salt-textured color. The detail of the scarf on the left was created by painting a light green ground, leaving white areas for a future application of color. Once the ground color was dry, Joan utilized line-building techniques to establish her design. Afterward she added the yellow-orange salt texture to the white areas.

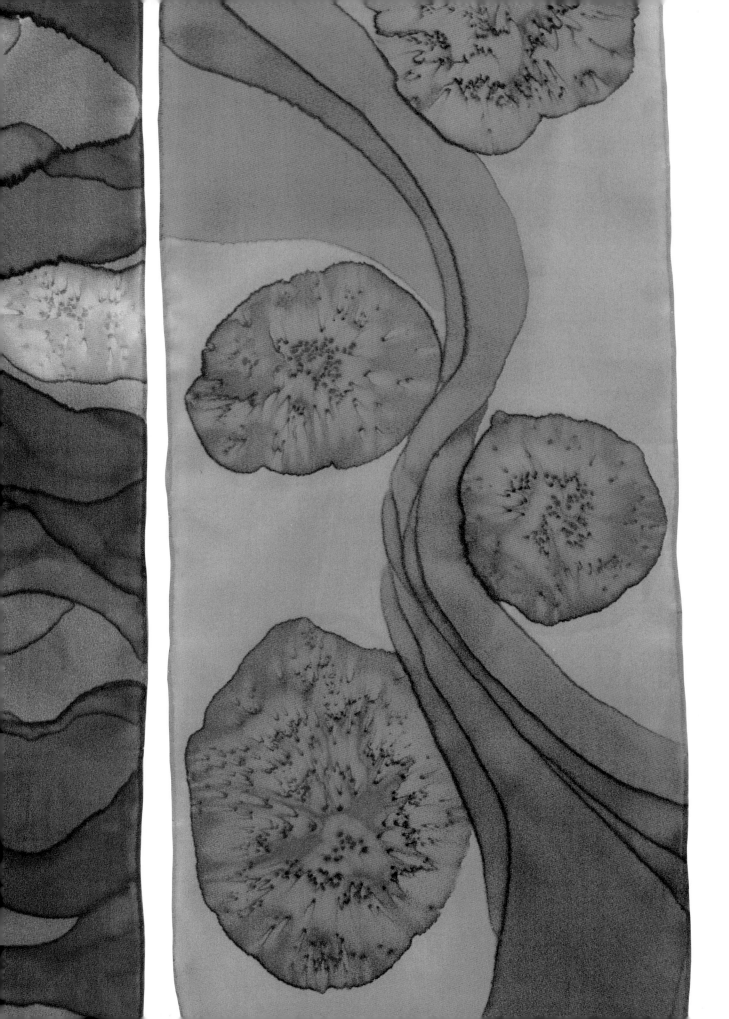

DEMONSTRATION:
Line Building

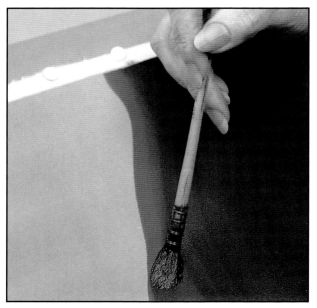

Paint a light ground color and let it dry. Then paint a shade slightly darker than the ground color, partially covering it. Let at least one edge of the shade dry naturally on the silk.

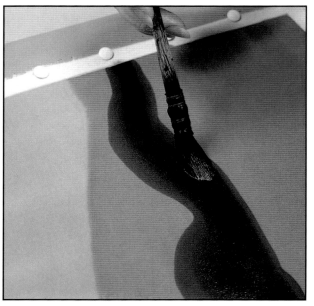

Begin to build up layers of overlapping shades. In this example each shade is darker than the one before. Most designs work best if each shade covers a subsequently smaller area of the ground.

Here you can see layers starting to form a design. Note how much the two layers shown in the first two photographs have lightened as they dried.

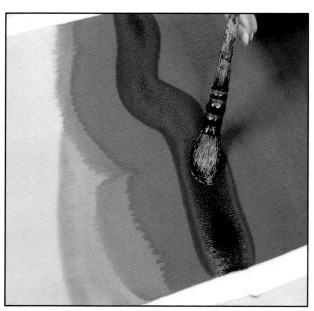

Work your way down the silk, one layer at a time. The dye sometimes creates interesting effects as it dries. If you like what you see, you can halt the flow of the dye with a hair dryer.

Here is the final effect when the silk is dry. The look is much like tree-covered mountains receding into the distance.

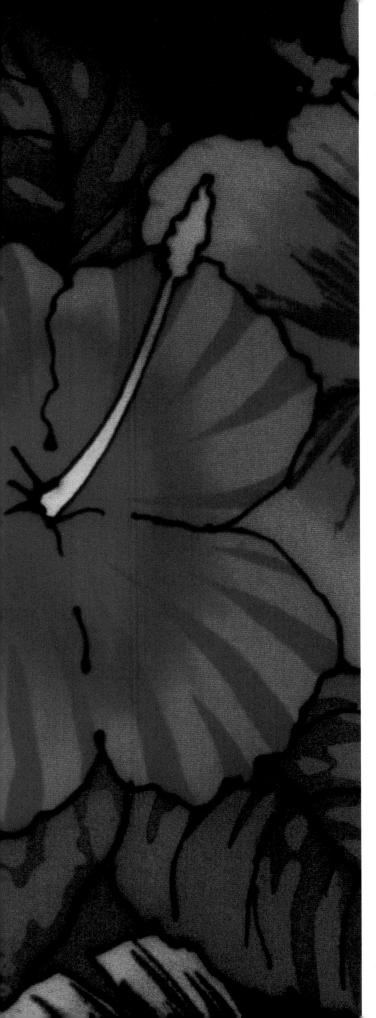

10: COMBINING TECHNIQUES

One of the marvelous things about silk painting is that different techniques can be combined, or layered, in the same piece to create very subtle and exciting effects. From my teaching perspective I find that students who begin to experiment with layering one color on top of another—or one technique on top of another—open the door to many creative possibilities for self-expression. Their design work becomes more integrated and painterly, their color schemes are more harmonious and unique, and they begin to generate more ideas and accomplish more work outside the class. Yet, oddly, it is rare to see a silk painting that incorporates several of the techniques described in this book.

Learning to layer colors and combine techniques is an exciting transition for a silk painter. This section is intended as a guide for those beginning to experiment with these processes. The silk paintings reproduced here are examples of work that used these principles successfully.

Hibiscus Flame. © Sissi Siska.

THE LAYERING PROCESS

The process of successive applications of resists and dye is what silk painters refer to as layering. Layering is not a specific technique but a combining of the various techniques involved in silk painting.

Because of the diversity and nature of wax and gutta resist techniques, there are several ways to approach layering. Many of the silk paintings in this book were done by layering, and each artist combines various techniques to create a unique, expressive style. See, for example, *Leland's Garden* on page 1. Sissi Siska was one of the original surface designers to develop patterns on silk for the trade. *Leland's Garden* incorporates clear gutta, black gutta, wax, and various painting and overdyeing techniques.

Joanne Siska worked in wax resist and several painting techniques to create *Coral Reef* on pages 10–11. First she waxed out areas on the white silk for future development of the fish. The background motifs were then painted by successive applications of dye and wax. The dye was applied using wet-on-wet alcohol techniques, and the waxed areas were applied to resist the dye, preserving the original color. The background was then steam-fixed and the wax subsequently removed during the steaming process. To paint the fish, Joanne first applied wax around the white areas so that she could apply the dye without the risk of color bleeding into other areas. To create the fish Joanne used successive applications of wax and painting techniques such as shading and blending to build form and detail. After a second steaming, Joanne applied gutta treatment to areas of the painting, which allowed her to add more details and refine her fish.

The artwork featured here plus the step-by-step illustration of working with layers of color and wax on treated silk will help you understand the creative and technical possibilities. A fuller understanding and individual design direction will unfold as you begin to practice and experiment with your own designs and ideas on silk.

TIPS

The following list of helpful hints is in response to the questions, technical observations, and problems encountered while working with gutta, hot wax resists, and dyes during the process of layering.

• The color scheme will be very harmonious if the resist is applied on a colored ground. The ground color can be flat, shaded, ombré, variegated, or a visual texture. Always apply the lightest color first, building up layers to a deeper or darker color.

• Hot wax can be applied over dry-cleanable black and colored guttas. *Caution:* If you use a hot iron to remove wax, some of the colored gutta may be absorbed by the newsprint. If the silk is then shifted and ironed further, the unwanted colored gutta will transfer back onto the silk. To avoid this, keep a fresh layer of newsprint next to the silk, and iron carefully.

• Since gutta lines will not penetrate treated silk, use beeswax and an electric wax applicator for applying a linear resist on treated silk.

• When mixing colors by overdyeing on the silk, a general rule is to apply no more than three medium to strong applications of different colors. A fourth application will produce a muddy color, unless the dyes are diluted or the colors are very closely analogous. (Similar advice holds true for any medium that has a translucent quality, like watercolor, colored pencils, and silk painting.) After about five applications of dye, the original gutta resist lines may deteriorate because of the alcohol in the dilutant.

• Silk fibers have a saturation point and will receive only so much dye. Therefore the number of color layers that can be overpainted depends on the strength of the dye and the weight of the silk. If too much dye is applied, the color may travel across the resist barriers during the steaming process, especially superconcentrated dyes on heavy-weight silk such as undiluted Super Tinfix orchid and bergamote yellow.

• When gutta is applied over a color or salt residue, make sure it is penetrating the silk properly. This is especially true with heavy-weight silks, which soak up a lot of color. The silk becomes heavier and stiffer with every application of dye. If needed, adjust to this by thinning the gutta with a solvent.

• During the successive applications of dye, a small amount of the ground color may migrate to the resist barriers, creating a dark edge. Most silk painters find this a desirable effect. To help eliminate dark edges and possible streaking when overpainting, some silk painters steam-set their ground color before applying the resist and a second application of color. Once the dye is fixed, it will not migrate or streak when overpainted.

• Gutta and wax will not always retain their resist qualities through the process of steam-fixing.

• For overpainting use gutta rather than water-based resists. Gutta's delicate linear barrier will hold up under successive applications of dye, but water-based resists easily break down. Also, some water-based resists tend to remove color when they are rinsed out of the fabric, leaving light lines around motifs and backgrounds.

Patterns of Movement (detail from a kimono). © Margaret and
Glenn Jackson. This detail of a kimono incorporates gutta resist
with ground colors, ombré, shading, overpainting, and alcohol
techniques.

Peggy and Glenn start a design project, such as this exquisite kimono, by working out a tight cartoon sketch of their design. His influence is the geometric patterns and hers is the linear florals. The
design stage is the only premeditated part of Peggy's silk-painting
process. The rest is an improvised dance with the dyes, silk, and
resist derived from her experience with the medium.

To build a ground to paint over, Peggy started in the center of
the design and applied a subtle ombré of light cream that became
slightly darker as it reached the outer edges. Since dyes do not
travel as much on a heavy-weight charmeuse as they do on a lightweight silk, Peggy was able to control the subsequent applications
of salmon and emerald without the use of a resist.

Once she laid in all her ground colors, she worked back and
forth simultaneously with the gutta and dye to build up both the
geometric divisions and floral motifs. As she worked she manipulated the dye on the silk with alcohol dilutant to create a variety of
visual effects, integrating her design by overpainting her initial
ground colors.

Combining Techniques • 123

DEMONSTRATION:
Layering with Gutta

This layering exercise was executed by Jane Kosminsky.

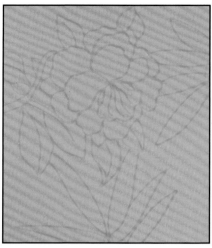

First she applied the gutta motif over a dry ground color.

Next she painted in the shaded motif.

Surface design © Julie Jennings. To execute this design, Julie used gutta resist and incorporated ombré, shading, overpainting, and alcohol techniques.

Julie has worked with many tropical motifs, so she has a repertoire of images that she understands and is able to apply to the silk in her unique freehand style. To execute this design in gutta, Julie placed her flowers first, then drew the foliage integrating the fish, and then added her background patterns. Next she applied the first layer of shading and ombrés to the white silk.

Once the silk was dry, Julie worked backed into her images to give them more form and interest. For example, the fish were first painted in a ombré; then Julie outlined the dots, squiggles, and stripes in gutta and overpainted the ground colors with a darker blue to bring out these shapes.

Then she added a layer of bright blue to the background around the motif.

After the background had dried, Jane outlined the background leaves with gutta.

To highlight the leaves, she layered a deeper shade of blue around the bright blue leaves. She could also have created a shadow effect by painting the leaves dark blue and leaving the background bright blue.

Surface design © Julie Jennings. This design incorporates gutta resist with flat color, overpainting, and shading techniques.

First the images and background patterns were drawn with gutta on a white ground. Julie then painted the leaves in various flat colors, used the alcohol technique to shade the flowers, and applied an ombré to the fish. Once the silk dried, Julie worked back into the ground colors. For example, Julie created the illusion of form in the flatly painted central leaf by first delineating its veins with gutta lines and then, when overpainting, shading the leaf from dark to light between those lines. Notice how the gutta lines within the leaf almost disappear into the form.

Dolphins (detail). © Julie Jennings. This tropical painting incorporates gutta resist, ombré grounds, and overpainting.

First Julie delineated the garland of flowers, the horizon, and the tops of the dolphins with gutta line on a white ground. She then painted the garland yellow, the horizon an ombré of blue to orange, the ocean an ombré of blue to violet, and from the dolphin line down she painted an ombré of blue to green to yellow.

After the silk dried she delineated the rest of the dolphins plus the trees, leaves, mountains, and flowers in gutta line. Then Julie overpainted the garland in orange and the dolphins and leaves in blue. Once the silk was dry, she applied a third layer of gutta and overpainted a dark blue dye to the underside of the dolphins and a deeper red-orange to the garland of flowers.

Golden Batik Orchids. *© Sissi Siska. For this surface design Sissi incorporated permanent black gutta and wax resist with faux batik, overpainting, and shading techniques.*

Sissi delineated her flowers and some of the foliage in the foreground in black gutta on a white ground. After she painted and shaded the motifs in several colors, she worked back into them with various wax brushstrokes. Before overpainting she selectively added faux batik for textural interest by applying and cracking the wax on the orchids. The background was first painted in a deep red, and then the palm leaves were suggested with strokes of wax that were brought to life when the background was overpainted with black dye.

DEMONSTRATION:
Layering on Treated Silk

This sequence demonstrates how a wax resist opens new design possibilities when it is applied to treated silk.

Green dye is painted directly onto treated silk. Notice how painting dye on the treatment is similar to painting on paper: The dye does not flow.

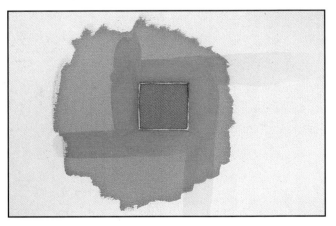

To trap a color in the white square and to protect the green from subsequent applications of dye, brushstrokes of hot wax are applied over the green and around the white square.

Coral dye is then painted in the square. The wax prevents the coral from bleeding into the green and vice versa.

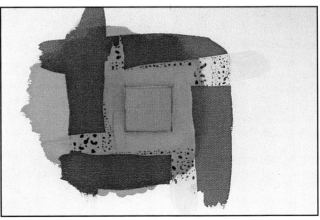

Brushstrokes of brown dye are applied over the wax and green dye, making the wax brushstroke an integral part of the motif.

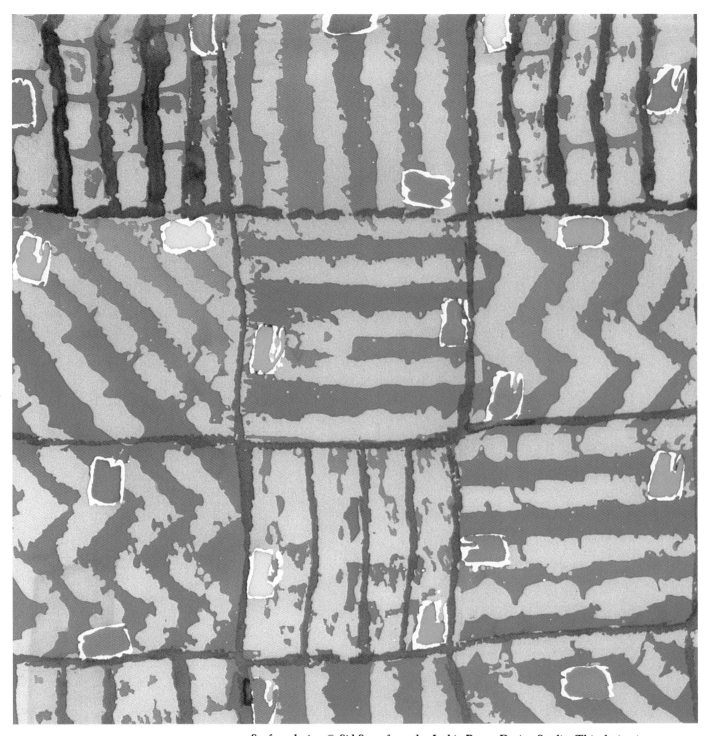

Surface design © Sid Scott from the Jackie Peters Design Studio. This design incorporates treated silk, wax resist, and the technique of overpainting with a sponge.

In order to paint directly on the silk without the use of a linear barrier resist, Sid prepared his silk with gutta treatment (a solution of gutta and solvent). Once the treatment was thoroughly dry, Sid painted the small shapes of color you see scattered throughout the design. To protect the colors he applied wax over the shapes, catching a white edge for extra protection and visual interest. The surrounding area was then painted a light periwinkle.

After the silk dried, Sid applied wax resist stripes and zigzags and then overpainted the unwaxed areas in a medium shade of violet. After carefully ironing the wax out of the design, Sid used a sponge to apply a dark color to accentuate the grid of squares.

Tiger Flower. © Joanne Siska. This very spirited design was executed with hot wax and incorporates the wet-on-wet, overpainting, and alcohol techniques.

Joanne suggested the shapes of her leaves and flowers with wax on a white ground. Then she built the image of each flower. In order to control the dye and avoid hard-edged lines of color, Joanne applied an alcohol dilutant to the white ground. Then working wet-on-wet, Joanne applied the dye.

Once the silk dried, Joanne waxed in the shape of the flower. She continued this process, applying one color at a time, letting the color dry, and then waxing in the image. After completing the building of all her motifs, she overpainted the background in black.

Abstract Triangles. © Joanne Siska. Joanne treated her white silk with a gutta solvent solution so that she could use a triangular cosmetic sponge to apply the dye directly to the fabric. When black dye is overpainted on colors that have been applied to treated silk, especially the hot colors, the black often fuzzes. To avoid this technical problem, Joanne intermittently steamed her design to set the colors before applying the black. Since Joanne works on several designs simultaneously she can efficiently steam-set her ground colors while working on other designs. Once the dye was steam-set, she applied brushstrokes of wax, overpainted the unwaxed areas with black dye, and set the black in a final steaming.

Surface design © Joanne Siska. This design is executed in wax resist and incorporates wet-on-wet, shading, overpainting, and alcohol techniques.

First Joanne outlined the white leaves and flowers with a brush and hot fluid wax on a white ground. Then she painted in many of her colors, working over an alcohol dilutant base. Notice how she often painted her ombrés and shades of color up against the wax resist, letting the dye flow to a soft edge. Once the dye was dry, Joanne created detail in the leaves and flowers as she applied wax to the rest of her images.

When the images were complete, Joanne painted in a flat blue background. Once the ground was dry she created small leaf shapes with brushstrokes of wax resist and applied a darker blue over the lighter blue ground to bring out the shapes of the leaves.

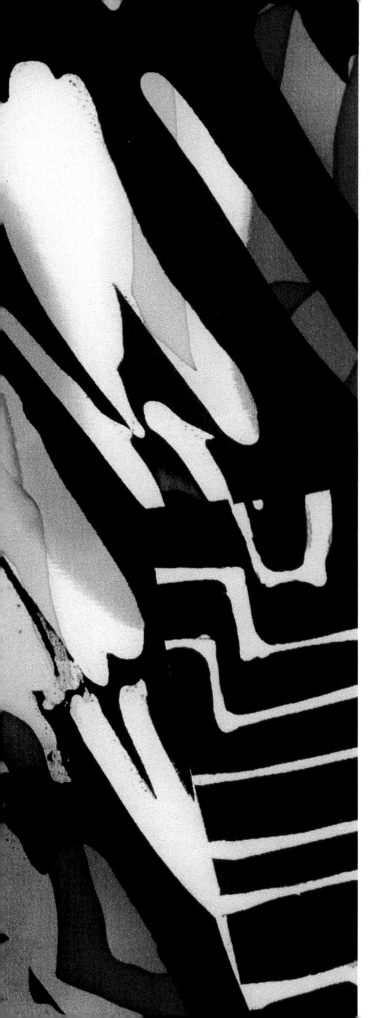

11: FINISHING PROCESSES

When a silk painting is complete, it is time for the crucial process of steam-fixing the dye to the fabric. The steaming process not only sets the dye permanently and bonds it with the silk, but also develops the color to bring out all its brightness and intensity. Any gutta or wax residue that remains in the painting after it is steam-fixed can be removed by having the silk dry-cleaned. After the silk is dry-cleaned it should be rinsed in a bath of clear water to remove any excess dye. Once you have completed the finishing processes, the silk will regain its natural softness and luster, and your design will have become an integral part of the silk.

Surface design © Jackie Peters from the Jackie Peters Design Studio.

STEAM FIXING

Once the dyes are fixed and bonded with the silk, a painting can be washed with care or dry-cleaned. The method of fixing depends on the chemistry of the dyes. Check the method required before purchasing dyes.

French dyes (Tinfix, Super Tinfix, and H. Dupont) and Jacquard silk colors require steam fixing. During the process of steaming, the heat and moisture penetrate the dyes to create a concentrated dye bath, which bonds the dyes to the silk. Jacquard silk colors can be washed in a fixative bath that helps set the dyes and removes excess color. To develop their colors to the fullest, however, these dyes should also be steam-fixed.

Dry cleaning, followed by rinsing and ironing, put the final touches on a silk painting and bring out all its natural beauty.

You can purchase a steamer from a supplier or assemble one yourself very simply and inexpensively out of a stovepipe, a coat hanger, and a pasta pot. A 2-foot (61-cm) stovepipe will accommodate long scarves and paintings up to 14 inches (36 cm) wide. A 5-foot (152-cm) stovepipe will accommodate large paintings and yards of 45-inch (114-cm) fabric. A stovepipe 8 inches (20 cm) in diameter will accommodate a roll of silk 5 to 6 inches (15 to 18 cm) thick, still leaving enough room between the outer edge of the hanging roll and the inner surface of the pipe.

Assembling Your Own Stovepipe Steamer

If you decide to build your own stovepipe steamer instead of buying one, here are the supplies you will need:

- *Galvanized stovepipe*, 8 inches (20 cm) in diameter, which can be purchased through a local plumbing and heating supplier. For more efficient steam and heat penetration, some silk painters wrap a layer of glass wool insulation around the outside of the pipe, keeping the insulation above the water line and securing it with duct tape.
- *Wire clothes hanger* to suspend the roll of fabric in the pipe.
- *Tin snips* to cut the wire and stovepipe.
- *Heavy-weight pasta pot* that will hold the water and support the stovepipe.
- *Teakettle* or extra pot for boiling water.
- *Efficient hot plate* that will bring water to a boil. A hot plate that has two burners spaced far enough apart to accommodate the large pot and a teakettle would be ideal.
- *Newspaper*, and *cotton towel*, to absorb moisture and steam during the steaming process.

Rolling the Silk

Once you have put together the stovepipe steamer itself, you will need a few more readily available supplies for rolling the silk. First of all you will need a roll of 48-inch (122-cm) newsprint or porous brown wrapping paper (not shiny). The paper you choose should be porous enough to allow steam to penetrate. To steam six yards (549 cm) of 44-inch (112-cm) fabric, you will need 8 yards (732 cm) of 48-inch (122-cm) paper. A roll of brown wrapping paper can be reused for several steamings, but newsprint becomes too flimsy and stained to reuse.

You will also need a few miscellaneous items: heavy-duty aluminum foil; masking tape; newsprint, either large sheets

(24 by 36 inches; 61 by 91 cm) or a roll; newspaper, a tape measure, pot holders; and two silk clips or clothespins.

The roll of fabric should hang in the center of the stovepipe. If the roll rests against the pipe, it will collect condensation, which will stain the design. Therefore, the 1-inch (2.5-cm) notches that support the rod must be directly across from each other in the top of the pipe. To determine the location of the notches, measure the pipe's circumference with a tape measure and divide the circumference in half. Use a pair of tin snips to cut two rectangular flaps, one on each side of the pipe, approximately 1 inch (2.5 cm) deep and ¼ inch (.6 cm) wide. Fold the flaps of cut metal down flat inside the pipe.

The wire that supports the roll of fabric will pass through the notches, lie across the top, and hang down the outer sides of the stovepipe. To make it, use the tin snips to cut and bend the clothes hanger into a U shape so the bottom of the U fits over the diameter of the pipe. (See the photo on page 136.)

Caution: Refer to the list of special precautions for steaming on page 137 before rolling your silk.

PREPARING THE SILK FOR STEAMING

1. Make a support tube for the center of the roll by rolling several tight revolutions at the begining of the porous paper.
2. Position and roll the first piece of silk in the paper, maintaining a 2-inch (5-cm) border of paper at the top to provide space for the wire hanger to pass through. Leave at least a 1-inch (2.5-cm) border at the bottom of the roll. Add one piece of silk at a time so that none of them touch each other but are separated by paper. As the silk is rolled into the paper, continuously smooth out any creases and check the ends of the roll to be sure they are even. Roll at least seven or eight times past the end of the last piece of silk. As you lay out additional pieces of silk, use silk clips or clothespins on the ends of the roll to keep the roll tightly wrapped. Once the silk is rolled, do not tap the ends of the roll to make them even. This will twist the silk, causing lightweight silk to ripple. Subsequent steaming may set the ripples.
3. Mark "top" on the end with the 2-inch (5-cm) border. Tape the loose flap closed in a few places with masking tape.
4. Make a jacket of two layers of heavy-duty aluminum foil to seal and cover at least 6 inches (15 cm) of the bottom end of the roll. Seal the jacket to the roll with tape. Make sure that the tape is flush to the roll—that is, flat against it with no creases—so that condensation will not collect and seep through the paper.
5. Punch a hole in the 2-inch (5-cm) border, 1 inch (2.5 cm) from the top of the roll, and insert the support wire. Make another hole directly across and pull the wire through. Make sure the holes are centered and across from each other so that the roll will hang straight in the pipe.
6. Carefully, so that the foil does not rip, slide the roll of fabric into the stovepipe and suspend it from the top by placing the wire into the notches.
7. Place the pipe in the pot on the hot plate and add 1½ to 2 inches (4 to 5 cm) of water to the pot. If you have followed the directions, there should be about 10 inches (25 cm)

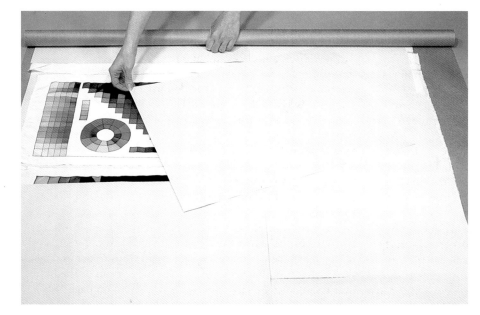

In preparation for steaming, the color chart is placed between sheets of newsprint and then tightly rolled in porous brown paper.

The bottom of the roll is protected from the boiling water and condensation by taping and sealing heavy aluminum foil flush across the end of the roll and several inches up its sides.

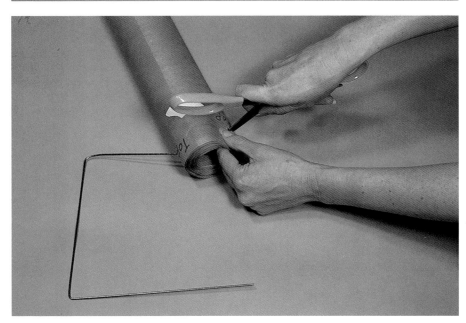

A hole is punched through the top of the roll, and the support hanger is slipped through to hold the roll in place while another hole is punched through the paper directly across from the first.

between the water line and the roll of silk. This space serves as a buffer so that the roll will not be splashed by boiling water.

8. Use aluminum foil to enclose the gap between the pot and the pipe. Leave a flap for loosening the foil for subsequent additions of boiling water to the pot.

9. To absorb excess moisture, cover the top of the pipe with a layer of newspaper ¾ inch to 1 inch (2 to 2.5 cm) thick and a thick cotton towel.

10. Weight down the top with a fabric weight or brick. *Caution:* Make sure the floor, hot plate, and pot are level and the pipe is properly supported before putting a weight on the top of a stovepipe steamer. If the pipe is not balanced properly, the weight may fall off.

11. Do not let the pot boil dry, or your paintings will burn and discolor. Check the water level periodically and refill the pot with boiling water as needed. *Caution:* Just in case you bump the pot when refilling it, remove the weight from the top of the stovepipe so that it cannot fall off and hurt you. The replace it when the water has been added.

12. Steam for 3 to 4 hours. (Refer to the chart of dye characteristics on pages 140–143.)

13. When removing the roll from the stovepipe, handle the hot pipe with pot holders.

Once the support hanger is in place, the rolled fabric is carefully slipped into the stovepipe and suspended from the two notches in the top of the pipe. The roll should be centered and hang freely in the pipe without touching its sides.

The stovepipe is then placed in a heavy pot on the heating unit. At this point, check to make sure the stovepipe, heating unit, and heavy pot are level and balanced. This will keep the roll of silk correctly centered in the pipe so that it will hang straight down. Once you are sure the roll is not touching the sides, add about 2 inches of water to the pot, and close the gap between the pot and the pipe with heavy aluminum foil, leaving a flap for adding boiling water later. Cover the top of the pipe with a thick layer of newspaper and a cotton towel. Then secure it with a heavy weight.

SPECIAL PRECAUTIONS FOR STEAMING

When silk paintings are being steamed to set the dyes, they must be protected from staining one another and from being stained by condensation. Taking the following precautionary measures will help you avoid staining silk treated with the following substances:

Salt. Salt residue left in the silk will attract moisture that may cause the dye to bleed. Therefore, before rolling salt-treated silk with other work, remove any salt crystals that are stuck on the silk, and place the painting between several sheets of clean newsprint.

Wax. Wax will melt during the steaming process. To absorb the wax, layer wax-treated silk between sheets of clean newsprint and then three or four layers of newspaper. (Do not use newspaper directly against your paintings; the printers' ink may transfer and stain the design.) If the painting has a heavy layer of wax, some of it can be removed before steaming by first ironing it between two sheets of newsprint.

Strong dyes. Strong concentrations of dye may transfer during the steaming process. Extra layers of newsprint rolled with the design will absorb the excess dye.

Gutta and gutta-like resists. Gutta may stick to the newsprint, but the bits of paper that stick to the clear gutta will be removed during dry cleaning. Place paintings that incorporate metallic gutta-like resists, which are not dry-cleanable, between sheets of lightweight cotton muslin.

To avoid steam-setting creases, smooth the fabric as it is being rolled. To remove any creases that do occur, rinse and iron the silk while it is still damp. You may need to repeat the procedure a few times.

The amount of time needed to steam-fix the dyes varies. To determine the time, take into consideration the weight of the silk, the concentration of dye, the amount of yardage, and the equipment you are using. For example, if you are steaming one or two scarves in the stovepipe steamer, it will take approximately 2 hours to set most colors, and 3 hours for concentrated colors or rich blacks. Steaming yardage of 14-momme to 16-momme crepe de chine in a stovepipe steamer will take approximately 2 to 3 hours for paintings and 4 hours for wearable art.

To establish the amount of time required to steam wearable art, include a test piece of painted fabric in the roll of fabric to be steamed. The test piece should be placed in the beginning of the roll. After steaming for about the right amount of time, rinse the test piece in a bowl of cool water. If an excess of dye runs or continues to bleed from the design, reroll the silk in the opposite direction so that the center of the roll is now on the outside, and vice versa. Then continue to steam

the roll of silk for at least an additional hour. As you gain experience you will be able to easily gauge the appropriate amount of time.

Suppliers recommend steaming Jacquard silk color dyes for 30 to 40 minutes. However, a longer steaming time may be required to penetrate the inside of a thick roll.

When steaming a large heavy roll in a production or class situation, there are a few steps that should be taken to ensure success. Make sure the stovepipe is large enough to allow the steam to circulate. Stovepipes come in 10-inch (25-cm) diameters. A 6- to 7-inch (15- to 18-cm) roll in a 10-inch (25-cm) pipe would allow 1½ to 2 inches (4 to 5 cm) for steam to circulate properly; a larger roll would be too thick.) Before rolling the silk, reinforce the porous wrapping paper by running masking tape along the rim of the 3-inch (8-cm) border. Use a heavy-duty rod to suspend the fabric in the pipe. Invert an extra large, stainless steel vegetable steamer into the bottom of the pipe. (The upside-down steamer will keep the roll from falling into the water if it happens to dislodge from the rod.) Finally, adjust the steaming time so that the center of the roll is fully steamed.

DRY CLEANING

After the painting has been steamed, it should be dry-cleaned to remove any clear gutta or wax. You can have your silk paintings professionally dry-cleaned or do it yourself using a cleaning fluid such as Afta, manufactured by Guardsman, available at your local hardware store. The dry cleaning will also remove any stiffness and bring back the soft, pliant hand of the silk.

When dry-cleaning a painting that contains black dye or black dry-cleanable gutta, you should take steps to prevent the gutta from smearing and the dye from staining when it comes into contact with other areas of the silk. Layer each painting between sheets of lightweight fabric, such as China silk or cotton sheeting. To secure them, use safety pins or staples, or run a basting stitch along the edges. The protective sheets can be washed and reused.

RINSING

Wearable art that was executed with black or metallic gutta and that does not require dry cleaning to remove gutta or wax should be rinsed in water to remove any excess dye and to bring back the silk's natural softness and pliancy. It is best to wait 48 hours after steaming; then rinse the silk in three to four successive tubs of cold water until the water runs fairly clear. Do not twist or wring the silk or leave it in a heap. To neutralize any traces of alkali, in the next to the last rinse, add a tablespoon of pure white vinegar to each quart of water. Roll the silk in a clean towel and then hang or lay it flat on top of a clean towel to dry. Towels used for this may become stained, but they can be washed and reused.

Ironing the silk while it is still damp gives it a pleasingly soft hand and brings up the color.

LIST OF SUPPLIERS AND MAIL-ORDER CATALOGS

Atelier de Paris
Mailing address:
1556 S. Fairfax Ave.
Los Angeles, CA 90019

Showroom:
1543 South Robertson Blvd.
Los Angeles, CA 90035

(213) 553-6636
Fax (213) 931-7474

H. Dupont dyes, dye kits, gutta, stretcher frames, silks and silk scarves, squirrel-hair quill brushes, foam brushes, Synthrapol, steaming paper, steaming service.

Cerulean Blue Ltd.
P.O. Box 21168
119 Blanchard St.
Seattle, WA 98111-3168

(206) 443-7744
Fax (206) 443-4735

Chinese wash brushes, metal-tipped fine-line applicators for gutta, fiber-reactive dyes, wax resists, silks, hand-cleaning paste, squeeze bottles, shinshi.

David Davis
Fine Art Materials Inc.
346 Lafayette St.
New York, NY 10012

(800) 237-0061
(212) 982-7100

H. Dupont dyes; gutta; all types of brushes, including squirrel-hair quill; fabric steamers. Will mail phone orders.

Dharma Trading Co.
P.O. Box 916
San Rafael, CA 94915

(800) 542-5227
(415) 456-7657

Tinfix, Super Tinfix, and Jacquard dyes; silk fabrics and scarves; gutta and metal-tipped gutta applicators; wax resists; sable, foam, and Chinese wash brushes; silk clips; fabric steamers.

Horikoshi New York
55 West 39th St.
New York, NY 10018

(212) 354-0133

Fine Japanese silk, wool challis, silk scarves. May have minimum order; call for an appointment.

Ivy Craft Imports
5410 Annapolis Rd.
Bladenburg, MD 20710

(301) 779-7079
Fax (301) 779-5791

Tinfix and Super Tinfix silk dyes, dye kits, gutta and metal-tipped gutta applicators, silks and silk scarves, frames, foam and squirrel-hair quill brushes, fabric steamers and steaming paper, squeeze bottles.

New York Central Art Supply Company
62 Third Ave.
New York, NY 10003

(212) 477-0400
(800) 950-6111

Tinfix and Super Tinfix dyes, gutta and gutta applicators, squirrel-hair quill brushes.

Pearl Paint
308 Canal St.
New York, NY 10013

(212) 431-7932
(800) 221-6845

Tinfix and Super Tinfix Dyes, Jacquard silk colors, gutta and gutta applicators, watercolor rounds, silks and silk scarves.

Pro Arte
P.O. Box 1043
Big Timber, MT 59011

(406) 932-5228
(800) 736-5234

Watercolor rounds made of Prolene fiber and a combination of squirrel-hair and Prolene.

Pro Chemical and Dye Inc.
P.O. Box 14
Somerset, MA 02726

(508) 676-3838
Fax (508) 676-3980

Fiber-reactive dyes, electric tjanting, waxes, Synthrapol.

Quailin International
P.O. Box 31145
San Francisco, CA 94131

(415) 647-1329

Silk fabrics and scarves.

Rupert, Gibbon and Spider, Inc.
P.O. Box 425
Healdsburg, CA 95448

(800) 422-0455
(707) 433-9577
Fax (707) 433-4906

Jacquard silk colors, gutta and metal-tipped gutta applicators, wax resists, silk fabrics and scarves, Synthrapol, squirrel-hair quill brushes, foam brushes, stretcher frames, fabric steamers.

Silk Ltd.
The Apparel Center S1-159
350 North Orleans St.
Chicago, IL 60654

(312) 329-1670
(800) 222-SILK
Fax (312) 329-1635

Silks.

Silkpaint Corporation
Main office:
P.O. Box 18
18220 Waldron Dr.
Waldron, MO 64092

(816) 891-7774
Fax (816) 891-7775

Hawaii office:
47-194 Kam. Hwy.
Kaneohe, HI 96744
(808) 239-9299

H. Dupont dye.

Sureway Trading Enterprises
826 Pine Ave., Suites 5 and 6
Niagara Falls, NY 14301-1806

(416) 596-1887
(416) 596-8899
Fax (416) 596-7565

Tinfix, Super Tinfix, and H. Dupont silk dyes; Jacquard silk colors; gutta and metal-tipped gutta applicators; squirrel-hair quill brushes; foam brushes; silk fabrics and scarves.

Surma
11 East 7th St.
New York, NY 10003

(212) 477-0729

Electric wax pens and beeswax.

Testfabrics
P.O. Box 420
Middlesex, NJ 06846

(201) 469-6446

Silk and wool that has been degummed, scoured, and bleached so that it is ready for painting.

Textile Resources
123½ Main St.
Seal Beach, CA 90740

(231) 598-6652

Super Tinfix and H. Dupont dyes, Jacquard silk colors, gutta, gutta applicators, foam brushes, electric wax pens, waxes, Synthrapol, silks and silk scarves.

Thai Silks
252 State St.
Los Altos, CA 94022

(415) 948-8611
(800) 722-7455
In California,
(800) 221-SILK
Fax (415) 948-3426

Silks.

Savoir-Faire (Importers of Fine Materials for the Arts)
P.O. Box 2021
Sausalito, CA 94966

(415) 332-4660
Fax (415) 332-3113

Will provide information on art supply stores in your area that carry Super Tinfix and Tinfix dyes.

GLOSSARY

acid dye: a type of colorant that permanently stains protein fibers (silk and wool).

analogous colors: three to five neighboring hues on the color wheel.

blotch: a type of background where color is applied around the motif, versus the motif being overdyed on a ground.

complementary color: two hues found opposite each other on the color wheel.

color triads: three hues equidistant from one another on the color wheel.

color wheel: a circular color spectrum helpful for visualizing how colors interrelate.

designer: an artist who uses the elements of design (color, form, line, and texture) to create compositions.

diffusing agent: a liquid or chemical that helps dye mix and spread on silk.

dilutant: a liquid used to reduce the concentration of dye.

drape: a fabric's ability to fold, hang, and move with the body.

filament: a very slender thread.

finishing: washing, dry cleaning, and pressing of dyed fabric.

fixing: permanent attachment of dyes to silk fiber, usually accomplished by steaming.

ground: the foundation surface or background in a composition, applied before the motifs.

gutta-percha: a rubberlike substance obtained from the milky juice of the palaquium tree of Malaysia.

gutta resist: refined gutta-percha, used primarily as a linear barrier resist for the process of silk painting.

hand: the feel or tactile quality of a fabric, including body, drape, and touch.

hue: the name of a color, and one of its three measurable dimensions. *See also* intensity, value.

intensity: the brightness or dullness of a color, and one of its three measurable dimensions. *See also* hue, value.

isopropyl alcohol: a diffusing agent; also, a dilutant that helps keep dyes in solution.

metameric color: a condition in which different dyes or pigments appear identical under one kind of light (such as incandescent or fluorescent) but not under another (such as daylight).

momme (mm): a Japanese weight for silks. An 8-momme habutai silk weighs approximately 1 ounce per square yard.

monochromatic: containing different values and intensities of a single hue.

motif: the theme or dominant recurring visual element in a composition.

neutral: a gray, white, or black without identifiable hue. Neutrals match well with other colors or shades.

overdyeing: superimposing one or more dyes over a previously dyed fiber or fabric. If the dyes are transparent, they mix to create a new color.

ombré: soft gradations of one color into another.

print: a surface design on fabric.

process colors: the three subtractive primary colors used in printing: cyan, magenta, and yellow (also referred to as process blue, process red, and process yellow).

resist: a substance, such as wax or gutta, that prevents dye from penetrating specific areas of a silk painting.

shade: a deeper or darker value of a hue, obtained by adding black to the dye. *See also* tint, tone.

spectrum: white light separated into a series of colored bands by a prism. The colors appear in order of their respective wavelengths, from red (produced by the longest) to violet (produced by the shortest).

subtractive color mixing: a method of reproducing colors with dyes. The whole spectrum of colors can be created by combining a maximum of four colors: cyan, magenta, yellow, and black.

surface designer: one who creates designs that embellish the surface of fabric, papers, and objects.

Synthrapol: a mild soap manufactured specifically for removing excess dye after the dyes have been fixed to the fibers. It suspends and carries the dye from the fibers. It is also effective as a prewash to remove sizing from silk.

transparent color: a type of color (such as dye or watercolor) that allows light to pass through it. With transparent color, the white background serves as the only white; there is no such thing as a white dye.

tint: a paler or lighter value of a hue, obtained by adding white (dilutant) to the dye. *See also* shade, tone.

texture: the surface quality of materials; also, the visual or implied texture on the surface of silk (such as a salt texture).

tone: a middle value of a hue, obtained by adding gray (black plus dilutant) to the dye. *See also* shade, tint.

value: the amount of dark (black) or light (dilutant) in a color, and one of its three measurable dimensions. *See also* hue, intensity.

CHARACTERISTICS OF VARIOUS DYES

Several of the techniques demonstrated in this book rely on the behavior of the dye. For example, salt, alcohol, line building, shading and blending, and painting on treated silk work differently with some brands of dye than with others. It is helpful to know what to expect. However, if a technique produces an unforeseen reaction, the most versatile artists assist it—that is, see the creative potential in the behavior of the dye and use it to their advantage.

This chart is not meant to imply that one brand of dye is better than another. Rather, one brand may be more appropriate for a particular silk painting project or creative direction. For example, a fabric designer interested in the purest and most intense colors for swimwear design might prefer the Super Tinfix dyes; a surface designer creating and marketing wearable art may choose the Jacquard dyes for their washfast and colorfast qualities; a fine artist interested in creating painterly effects (textures, layering, alcohol techniques, and a range of rich premixed color) may choose H. Dupont or Tinfix. Also remember that the dye manufacturers continuously refine their products, so that the chemistry of each brand of dye may change over time. This may ultimately affect the dyes' affinity to specific techniques.

Other brands of dye are available besides those listed here. This chart will give you an idea of the qualities you should test for before deciding which dye to use for a given project. Nearly all dye manufacturers make small kits so that you can test and become familiar with the dyes without buying large quantities.

Salt, Alcohol, and Line-Building Techniques
Some brands of dye and some colors within a brand react with the fabric on contact, making it difficult or even impossible to manipulate the dye (push it around) on the silk. Therefore, you may want to test individual colors so that you are familiar with their behavior before planning your design or painting.

Lightfastness
Continuous exposure to light weakens silk. Commercially dyed silks that are fairly colorfast under most conditions will fade when exposed to direct sunlight. For this reason silk fabrics are not recommended for window treatments. Home furnishings made of painted silk, such as upholstery, pillows, and framed paintings, should be protected from exposure to direct sunlight. As with all fabrics, and some colors more than others, expect some fading over time.

Overdyeing
Generally, depending on the weight and weave of your silk, you can overpaint two to three intense hues or two hues plus black, and more if your colors are diluted (pastel tints) or closely analogous. After five applications of dye diluted with isopropyl alcohol, the gutta resist may begin to disintegrate.

Steaming
The steaming time for most dyes ranges from 15 to 45 minutes. But this is under industrial conditions that are difficult to duplicate. When you are steam-setting dyes at home or in a studio, the thickness of the rolled silk, the pressure in the steamer, the intensity of the dye, and the control of the temperature in the steamer are all variables that make it difficult to determine the amount of time it will take to set your dyes. Therefore, the French dye manufacturers and those silk painters who work with the dyes recommend 2 hours for paintings. 3 hours for intense black, and 3 to 5 hours for wearable art.

Theoretically you cannot oversteam; on the other hand, steamings that are more than 2 hours must be carefully monitored and the fabric protected so that condensation does not cause damage. (One way to prevent the steamer from cooling down is to add boiling water instead of cold water when the water level becomes low.)

BRAND OF DYE	DILUTANTS	SALT	Manipulating Dye with ALCOHOL
H. DUPONT (French)	Isopropyl alcohol and distilled water; H. Dupont dye thinner and distilled water; or Sennelier dye thinner and distilled water.	Beautiful effects possible. Dilute with alcohol dilutant.	Beautiful effects possible. Use alcohol or alcohol dilutant to manipulate dye.
SENNELIER TINFIX (French)	Isopropyl alcohol and distilled water; H. Dupont dye thinner and distilled water; or Sennelier dye thinner and distilled water.	Beautiful effects possible. Dilute with alcohol dilutant.	Test individual colors. Use alcohol or alcohol dilutant to manipulate dye.
SENNELIER SUPER TINFIX (French)	Isopropyl alcohol and distilled water; H. Dupont dye thinner and distilled water; or Sennelier dye thinner and distilled water.	Test individual colors. Primaries can be difficult, and altered colors work better than those straight from the bottle. Dilute with alcohol dilutant.	Test individual colors. Primaries can be difficult, and altered colors work better than those straight from the bottle. Use alcohol or alcohol dilutant to manipulate dye.
JACQUARD SILK COLORS	Distilled water; isopropyl alcohol and distilled water; H. Dupont dye thinner and distilled water; or Sennelier dye thinner and distilled water.	Test individual colors. Yellows and red can be difficult. Results more effective when isopropyl alcohol is added to dye.	Many of the colors react and bond with the fabric on contact, so test each color. Preplanning may be necessary. Dilute with isopropyl alcohol and distilled water before applying. Work quickly. Effect is improved if colors are mixed or overdyed. Use alcohol or alcohol dilutant to manipulate dye.

(chart continues on next page)

BRAND OF DYE	LINE BUILDING	OVERDYEING	SHADING and BLENDING
H. DUPONT (French)	Very effective.	Use H. Dupont or Sennelier dye thinner to make tints that will cover large areas such as backgrounds.	Most colors blend and shade easily. Use alcohol dilutant or H. Dupont or Sennelier dye thinner.
SENNELIER TINFIX (French)	Very effective.	Use Sennelier or H. Dupont dye thinner to make tints that will cover large areas such as backgrounds.	Most colors blend and shade easily. Use alcohol dilutant or H. Dupont or Sennelier dye thinner.
SENNELIER SUPER TINFIX (French)	Test individual colors; some build up darker ridges of concentrated dye than others.	Use Sennelier or H. Dupont dye thinner to make tints that will cover large areas such as backgrounds.	A few colors may be difficult to blend because they react with the silk on contact. When working with these colors, quickly rub your brush back and forth over the areas to be blended. Prolene watercolor, rounds are good for rub-blending. When blending and shading on a wet ground, use alcohol dilutant or H. Dupont or Sennelier dye thinner.
JACQUARD SILK COLORS	Test colors first. Not all will build up ridges of concentrated color.	Color may not be as pure as the French dyes, but beautiful colorations can be easily achieved. Colors that react and bond with the silk on contact tend not to streak when overpainted. Colors that do not bond immediately are more difficult to overpaint. For these colors, add dilutant to the dye, or wet the ground before overpainting. Use your brush to rub-blend any ridges of dye.	Many of these colors react with the silk on contact. To maintain a smooth transition when blending and shading, apply your colors to a damp-wet ground. Use distilled water, alcohol dilutant, or H. Dupont or Sennelier dye thinner.

Painting on TREATED SILK	STEAM-SETTING	COLORFASTNESS	LIGHTFASTNESS
Dilute dyes with alcohol dilutant.	Allow 2 hours for paintings, 3 hours for concentrated black, and 3–5 hours for wearable art.	Items such as small scarves that are easy to handle can be hand-washed with care. To avoid back-staining when working with large pieces of silk, dry cleaning is recommended. The dry-cleaning fluid does not disturb the color.	Keep out of direct sunlight. As with all dyes, some colors will fade more than others.
Dilute dyes with alcohol dilutant.	Allow 2 hours for paintings, 3 hours for concentrated black, and 3–5 hours for wearable art.	Items such as small scarves that are easy to handle can be hand-washed with care. To avoid back-staining when working with large pieces of silk, dry cleaning is recommended. The dry-cleaning fluid does not disturb the color.	Keep out of direct sunlight. As with all dyes, some colors will fade more than others.
Dilute concentrated dyes or they may bleed and become harsh or dull when steam-set. Unless you steam-set the dyes between applications, avoid using black over pure orchid, pergamote yellow, and other fugitive colors. The combination tends to bleed and fuzz during the steaming.	Allow 2 hours for paintings, 3 hours for concentrated black, and 3–5 hours for wearable art.	Items such as small scarves that are easy to handle can be hand-washed with care. To avoid back-staining when working with large pieces of silk, dry cleaning is recommended. The dry-cleaning fluid does not disturb the color.	Keep out of direct sunlight. As with all dyes, some colors will fade more than others.
Add a few drops of isopropyl alcohol to the dye. Alcohol acts as a solvent to help the dye penetrate the gutta treatment.	Although the manufacturer recommends 30 minutes of 212°F (100°C) steam heat to fix the dyes, you may want to run a test and adjust the timing to the amount of fabric being steamed and your steaming equipment.	Although the manufacturer promotes these dyes as exceptionally colorfast when steam-fixed, you may want to dry-clean highly constructed garments that could lose their shape if washed, or garments made from several yards of fabric.	These dyes have been formulated to be lightfast. Even so, don't expose to direct sunlight for long periods of time.

INDEX